ABSTRACTS OF WILLS AND ESTATES

O.C.R. Books V & VI

1852-1856

Vol. III

Barbour County, Alabama

Compiled by Helen S. Foley

SOUTHERN HISTORICAL PRESS INC.

Please direct all correspondence and orders to:

www.southernhistoricalpress.com
or
SOUTHERN HISTORICAL PRESS, Inc.
PO BOX 1267
375 West Broad Street
Greenville, SC   29601
southernhistoricalpress@gmail.com

ISBN #0-89308-183-3

Printed in the United States of America

Foreword

Barbour County, Alabama, was formed in 1832 from the Creek Cession of 1812 and from parts of Henry and Pike Counties. It was named for James Barbour, of Virginia.

The abstracts of wills and estates were taken from Orphans Court Records in the county probate office.

The administrators of estates and guardians of minors were required to present a yearly report at court. This included, in some instances, an itemized account of credits and debits and lists of items sold at the sale of personal property. For a guardian of a minor the "return" showed expenditures as board, schooling and financial credits due or paid by the estate of the minor. Often these lists were lengthy and could not be included in this abstract, thus a return was reported.

It was required that an inventory be made of the estate within thirty days after death and by that time an administrator was usually appointed.

The names of the decedents and persons appearing in court are arranged alphabically for Vol. V and again for Vol. VI of the O.C.R. (Orphans Court Records). Estates that did not reach a final settlement in these volumes are continued in later O.C.R. Books.

The names of administrators, guardians, witnesses and heirs are indexed in the back of the book.

O. C. R. BOOK V

Arrington, Elizabeth
> p. 90 Inventory and appraisal of the personal
> property of Elizabeth Arrington, dec'd. 24 Jan. 1853.
> p. 91. Elisha Arrington files list of property of
> the estate. 24 Jan. 1853.
> p. 94 Bond of Elisha Arrington as admr. of the
> estate of Elizabeth Arrington. Bondsmen: Thomas J.
> Head and Benjamin A. Barron. 20 Jan. 1853
> p. 220. Sale of personal property, Elisha Arrington,
> admr. 11 Apr. 1853.

Arrington, William
> pp. 197-200. Account current of the estate of William
> Arrington, Elisha Arrington, admr. 1 Feb. 1863.
> p. 219. Return of sale of perishable property ,
> Elisha Arrington, admr. 11 Apr. 1853.
> p. 395, Petition of Elisha Arrington to sell land for
> equal division to heirs, children of the dec'd. Heirs:
>> Elisha Arrington
>> Jeremiah Arrington, Wilkinson Co., Ga.
>> William Arrington
>> Francis Arrington
>> Amos Arrington
>> Harriet, wife of Elisha Hulin, Montgomery Co.
>> Elizabeth, wife of William Thomas
>> Emeline, wife of Allen Harp, Pike Co., Ala.
> 17 Sept. 1853
> p. 396-8. Authorized to sell land. 31 Oct. 1853.
> p. 616. Return of sale of real estate. 27 Mar. 1854.

Baker, James
> pp. 25-6 Final return of Seth Mabrey, guardian of:
>> William Baker, now 21 years old
>> Lydia Baker   Winney Baker
>> Margaret Baker   James Baker
> heirs of James Baker, dec'd. Mentions a sum of money
> to be paid over to the present guardian of Lydia,
> Margaret, Winney and James Baker. 11 Oct. 1852.
> p. 614. Return of Thomas S. Locke, guardian.
> 27 Mar. 1854.

Baker, Jeremiah
> p. 263. Annual return of F. E. Baker, guardian of:
>> Thomas E. Baker
> minor heir of Jeremiah Baker *. 19 Mar. 1853.
> pp. 605-6. Final settlement of F. E. Baker with his
> ward, Thomas E. Baker, who has attained his majority.
> 19 Dec. 1853.

* ABSTRACTS OF WILLS & ESTATES III: Estate of Jeremiah Baker.

Baker, Patience
        p. 429. Bond of Robert Baker and Aerial E. Jones as
admrs. of the estate of Patience Baker, dec'd. Bondsman: Jarrett Baker. 17 Nov. 1853.
        pp. 444-5. Inventory and appraisal of estate, A. E.
Jones, admr. 12 Dec. 1853.
        p. 445. Petition of Robert Baker and A. E. Jones,
admrs., for distribution of estate to heirs:
        Robert Baker
        Children of Emily Nichols, names and residences
            unknown
        Children of William Baker, S. C., names unknown
        Children of James Baker, dec'd., to-wit:
            Adeline Parmer   Peggy Baker, minor
            Enos H. Baker   Winney Baker, minor
            William Baker   James Baker, minor
            Lydia Baker, minor
        Mathew Baker, living in Ga.
        Nancy Wilson
        Jane Smith
        Elizabeth Tharp, living in Henry Co.
        Mary Prescott, living in S. C.
        p. 446. Commissioners appointed to divide proceeds
from the sale of personal property to heirs. Dec. 1853.
        pp. 540-1. Account of sale of personal property.
19 Jan. 1854.
        p. 577. Report of commissioners that the slaves can not
be equally divided without a sale. 15 Dec. 1853.
        p. 655. Return of sale of slaves. 13 Mar. 1854.

Barbour, Virgil
        pp. 433-4. Bond of Jaret P. Barbour as guardian of:
            Sarah Barbour
        minor heir of Virgil Barbour. Bondsman: Cornelius
Vorhees. 2 Dec. 1853.

Barnett, Thomas J.
        p. 134. Sale of perishable property, Mary A. Barnett,
admr. 15 Feb. 1853.
        p. 237. Heirs of Thomas J. Barnett:
            Julius C. Barnett   Sarah V. Barnett
            Mary O. Barnett   Thomas J. Barnett .
        all minor children of the dec'd., Mary Ann Barnett,
the widow, is admx. 23 May 1853.
        pp. 318-20. Annual settlement of Mary A. Barnett,
admx. 17 May 1853.
        p. 481. Bond of Mary A. Barnett as admx. of the estate.
Bondsmen: Thomas R. Sylvester and Henry P. Adams.
6 Jan. 1854.
        p. 541. Petition of Mary A. Barnett, admx., to keep
the estate together for the purpose of supporting the
family. Property consist of three houses in Eufaula,
one slave and 40 acres of land. 19 Jan. 1854.
        pp. 570-1. Return of Mary A. Barnett. 30 Nov. 1853.

Beauchamp, William *
> pp. 64-5. Return of Green Beauchamp, guardian of:
>
> Joseph S. Beauchamp   Henry W. Beauchamp
> Richard K. Beauchamp   Eliza J. Beauchamp
> Thomas H. Beauchamp
>
> p. 95. Division of slaves to heirs.
> pp. 170-1. Return of Green Beauchamp, guardian of
> the above named minors. 17 Jan. 1853.
> pp. 273-4. Final settlement of Green Beauchamp,
> guardian of Joseph S. Beauchamp, he has now arrived
> at the age of 21 years. 21 Feb. 1853.
> pp. 274-6. Return of Green Beauchamp, guardian.
> 18 Apr. 1853.

Beckham, Green C., minor
> p. 135. Final settlement of Thomas R. Sylvester,
> guardian of Green C. Beckham, minor heir of Rachel
> and Burrell Beckham **. The ward is now of the age
> of 21 years. 12 Feb. 1853.

Bellette, minors
> p. 176. Indenture between James Bullard and Probate
> Judge William R. Cowen to place James Bellette, an
> orphan about 3 years old, with James Bullard as an
> apprentice in brick masonry until he is 21 years old.
> 28 Mar. 1853.
> p. 176. Indenture between Mrs. Amanda Marahall and
> Probate Judge William A. Cowen to place Ella Bellette,
> an orphan about 6 years old, as an apprentice in the
> "business of housewifery" until she is 16 years old.
> 28 Mar. 1853.
> p. 177. Indenture between Mrs. M. J. Sneed and Probate
> Judge Wm. R. Cowen to place Pamelia Frances Bellette,
> an orphan about 9 years old, as an apprentice in the
> "business of housewifery" until she is 16 years old.
> 28 Mar. 1853.

Bennett, James
> p. 1. Nancy Bennett, widow of James Bennett, files her
> dissent to the Last Will and Testament. 22 Nov. 1852.
> p. 2. Bond of Nancy Bennett as excr. of the estate.
> Bondsmen: B. F. Pearson, Isiah Hancock, William A.
> Bennett, W. S. Webb, John W. Robertson, James A. Bennett,
> James A. Flournoy,John A. Reynolds and Eli F. Bennett.
> 9. Nov. 1852.
> pp. 87-8. Inventory and appraisal of the estate.
> 20 Dec. 1852.

* Continuation of ABSTRACTS OF WILLS & ESTATES II, III, IV.

** From: ABSTRACTS OF WILLS & ESTATES IV.

p. 89. Heirs of James Bennett:
　　Novel (Nevel?) Bennett, living in Ga.
　　Silas Bennett
　　Fanny Ann, wife of (John) Owens, living in Ga.
　　Sarah, wife of Charles Floyd, Chambers Co.
　　Louisa, wife of James Jones, Chambers Co.
　　Rachel J., wife of William S. Webb
　　Alexander Bennett, Macon Co.
　　Catherine, wife of James Fleming (Flournoy?)
　　　　living in Russell Co.
　　Eli F. Bennett
　　W. A. Bennett
　　Hariet E., wife of John Robinson, Macon Co.
　　Benjamin C. Bennett, minor
　　Julia Ann Bennett, minor
20 Dec. 1852.
pp. 119-21. Amount of sale of personal property.
12 Feb. 1853.
pp. 421-3. Petition of Nancy Bennett, excr., to sell
land for equal division to heirs, the same as above
with the exception:
　　Novel is listed as Nevel Bennett, Georgia
　　Catherine, wife of James Flournoy, Russell Co.
p. 428. Petition of Nancy Bennett, excr., for division
of personal property. 14 Nov. 1853.
p. 431. Bond of Nancy Bennett as excr. of the estate.
Bondsmen: Benjamin F. Pearson, J. M. Thornton, and
W. S. Webb. 21 Nov. 1853.
p. 630. Return of Nancy Bennett, excr. 21 Feb. 1854.

Benton, Dicy, minor
p. 105. Return of Daniel McKenzie, guardian of:
　　Dicy Benton *
17 Jan. 1853.
p. 616. Return of D. McKenzie, guardian. 27 Mar. 1854.

Bethune, James
p. 109. List of heirs of James Bethune, Elizabeth S.
Bethune, admr.
　　Julia E. wife of William Couch
　　Martha F., wife of L. F. Johnston
　　John S. Bethune　　　　　Sarah V.(Virginia)
　　Robert A. Bethune　　　　Bethune
　　Mary R. Bethune
　　Cornelia Bethune　　　　　William J. Bethune
All brothers and sisters of James Bethune, dec'd.
1 Feb. 1853.
pp. 207-8. Final settlement of the estate. 1 Feb. 1853.
Elizabeth Bethune, admx. List of heirs the same
as given above.

*　ABSTRACTS OF WILLS & ESTATES II: Dicy Benton was the
child of Mary Benton.

Bethune, William
     pp. 17-8. Final settlement of Richard S. Wright, guardian of:
          John S. Bethune
     heir of William Bethune, dec'd. He has now reached the age of 21 years. 25 Oct. 1852.
     p. 108. Return of Elizabeth S. Bethune, guardian of:
          Cornelia Bethune   Virginia Bethune
          William J. Bethune
     1 Feb. 1853.

Beverly, minors
     p. 78. Return of Daniel G. Beverly, guardian of:
          Mary J. Beverly   Christian Beverly
          Ann E. Beverly   William N. Beverly
     17 Jan. 1853.
     p. 540. Return of D. G. Beverly, guardian. 17 Jan. 1854.

Bishop, William
     p. 1.Bond of Sheppard M. Streeter as guardian of:
          Dixon H. L. Bishop
     minor heir of William Bishop. Bondsmen: B. D. Bishop and Council Bush. 6 Dec. 1852.
     pp. 19-21. Petition of Nancy Bishop, admx., to relinquish all her interest in the provisions of the will of her late husband, William Bishop *, for the benefit of her children, namely:
          Elizabeth, wife of William Blair
          Nancy, wife of T. S. Lightner
          James B. Bishop
          Wesley Bishop
          Emily, wife of Ryan Bennett
          William Bishop
          Rebecca, wife of Council Bush
          Jane, wife of Mathew M. Lassiter
          Dixon H. L. Bishop, minor
     9 Dec. 1852.
     pp. 68-71. Division of the estate into nine shares by commissioners appointed by the court. 20 Dec. 1852.
     p. 76. Petition of Nancy Bishop, admx., to sell real estate for equal division to heirs listed above. 20 Dec. 1852.
     pp. 109-10. List of personal and real estate. 3 Feb. 1853.
     p. 114. Authorized to sell land for division to heirs. 31 Jan. 1853.
     pp. 438-9. Bond of Wesley Bishop and Council Bush as admrs. of the estate. Bondsmen: A. E. Jones and J. B. Bishop. 12 Dec. 1853.

* ABSTRACTS OF WILLS & ESTATES II: Will of William Bishop.

pp. 527-8. Bill of appraisal of notes of the estate.
2 Jan. 1854.
p. 634. Return of Wesley Bishop, admr., on the sale of
land. 22 Feb. 1854.

Bizzell, Bennett
p. 115. Account of sale, W. A. Bizzell and A. W. Faulk,
admrs. of the estate of Bennet Bizzell *.
7 Feb. 1853.

Britt, Mathew
pp. 106-7. Petition of Thomas Flournoy, excr. of the
will of Mathew Britt **, that under the provisions of
the will the property is to be kept together for the
support and education of the children until they marry
or become of age. The testator left a number of slaves
and it is necessary to purchase land for additional
farming. The children need a guardian, they are in the
custody of their mother. Heirs are:
Elizabeth Britt, the widow
William R. Britt, age 21, non resident
Catherine V. Britt, minor
Mathew T. Britt, minor
Asa F. Britt, minor
Sarah Britt, minor
John T. Britt, minor
Moses Britt, minor
Henry D. Clayton appointed guardian ad Litem of minors.
19 Nov. 1853.
p. 116. Inventory of real estate purchased by Thomas
Flournoy, excr., for the benefit of the estate.
7 Feb. 1853.
p. 181. Sale of personal property, Thomas Flournoy,
excr. 28 Mar. 1853.
pp. 224-5. Elizabeth Britt, widow of Mathew Britt,
files her dissent to his will, which was probated on
21 June 1852. 26 Apr. 1853

Bryan, John
p. 658. Bond of John C. Bryan and William M. Bryan as
admrs. of the estate of John Bryan. Bondsmen: George
W. Cariker and Thomas J. Lasiter. 5 May 1854.

Bush, Charles D.
pp. 279-80. Bond of Seaborn J. Dubose and Selina B.
Bush as excrs. of the will of Charles D. Bush. Bondsmen: Jacob Parmer, E. S. Hoole, H. F. Reaves and

* Continued from ABSTRACTS OF WILLS & ESTATES BOOK IV.
** Will of Mathew Britt: ABSTRACTS OF WILLS & ESTATES IV.

William Williams. 13 June 1853.
pp. 280-1. Will of Charles D. Bush
    Wife: Selina B. Bush
    Children: Francis (Frances) Jane Bush
              Zachariah Bush
              Charles Dennis Bush
    Excrs: Selina B. Bush and Seaborn J. Dubose
    Wit: Jonathan Thomas, William G. Bush and Maria
        J. Thomas
    Date: 6 Apr. 1853
    Recorded: 13 June 1853.
pp. 304-8. Inventory of real and personal property,
Seaborn J. Dubose, excr. 11 July 1853.
pp. 447-8. Account of sales of personal property,
S. J. Dubose, excr. 12 Dec. 1853.
p. 651. Return of sales of cotton. 13 Mar. 1854.

Bush, Moses E. (Sr)
    p. 7. Final return of James Orr, guardian of:
    Moses E. Bush, (Jr.)
    minor heir of Moses E. Bush, (Sr.) *, He has now
    arrived at the age of 21 years. 19 Nov. 1852.

Bush, Zachariah
    p. 57. Bond of Charles D. Bush as guardian of Rutha
    (Ruth) C. Bush, minor heir of Zachariah Bush. Bonds-
    men: W. B. Crews and Anthony Windham. 27 Dec. 1852.
    p. 58. Bond of William G. Bush as guardian of Lucinda
    Bush, minor heir of Zachariah Bush. Bondsmen: Wright
    Flowers and Arthus Crews. 27 Dec. 1852.
    p. 67. Return of sale of land, William G. Bush, admr.
    19 Jan. 1853.
    p. 68. Return of William G. Bush, guardian of Lucinda
    Bush, minor. 19 Jan. 1853.
    p. 68. Return of Charles D. Bush, guardian of Ruth C.
    Thomas. 19 Jan. 1853.
    pp. 71-2. Division of property into nine shares to
    heirs. (Names of heirs given in final settlement).
    p. 77. Ruthy (Ruth) C. Thomas, minor, selects Charles
    D. Bush as her guardian. 27 Dec. 1852.
    p. 430. List of heirs given in final settlement with
    the exception: Mary, wife of John Watson, is listed in
    this document. 19 Nov. 1853.
    pp. 566-7. Account current of William G. Bush and the
    estate. 19 Nov. 1853.
    pp. 568-9. Final settlement of the estate to:
        Moses E. Bush
        Heirs of Charles D. Bush
        -----(Mary), wife of M. M. (John) Watson **
        W. G. Bush

*   ABSTRACTS OF WILLS & ESTATES III: Will of Moses E. Bush.
**   Barbour Co. Marriage Records: Mary R. Bush & John Watson
    married 10 Jan. 1850.

Ruth C., wife of Elliott Thomas
Mariah J., wife of Jonathan Thomas
Lucinda Bush, minor
Heirs of Retensey Thomas, dec'd., namely:
    Mary F. Thomas
    George H. Thomas   Zachariah T. Thomas
Heirs of Arincey Williams, dec'd., namely:
    Mary A. Williams   Jane A. Williams
    Columbianna Williams   Sarah E. Williams
    Louisianna Williams
9 Jan. 1854.

Campbell, Daniel
    pp. 339-40. Bond of Isaac H. Chambers and Paul McCall
    as admrs. of the estate of Daniel Campbell, dec'd.
    Bondsmen: Thomas F. Baxter and John P. McNair.
    10 Aug. 1853.
    p. 364. Inventory of real and personal property,
    Paul McCall, admr. 10 Oct. 1853.
    p. 461. Petition of Paul McCall and I. H. Chambers to
    sell personal property to pay debts of the estate.
    14 Dec. 1853.
    p. 517. Petition of Paul McCall and Isaac H. Chambers,
    admrs., to sell land in Pike Co., to pay debts of the
    estate. Heirs are:
        Neely Campbell, widow of the dec'd.
        Mary Ann Campbell
        City (Cathy) Ann Campbell *
        Nancy Campbell
        Cynthia Ann Campbell
        Duncan Campbell
        Ann Campbell
    10 Oct. 1853.
    p. 519. Authorized to sell land. 12 Dec. 1853.
    pp. 523-5. Petition of Neely Campbell, widow of Daniel
    Campbell, for dower, which is land lying in Barbour
    and Pike Counties.
    p. 526, Dower allotted to petitioner. 26 Nov. 1853.
    p. 544. Report of sale of personal property.
    23 Jan. 1854.
    p. 553. Return of sale of land. 9 Feb. 1854.
    p. 655. Return of sale of real estate, dower relinquish-
    ed in sale. 20 Mar. 1854.

Campbell, William D.
    p. 74. Final return of Paul McCall, guardian of:
        Joab (or Jacob) Campbell,
    heir of William D. Campbell, dec'd. He has now arrived
    at the age of 21 years. 19 Nov. 1852.

* U. S. 1850 Barbour County Census: Cathy Ann Campbell.

Carr, Thomas
> p. 399. Bond of Louisa C. Carr as admx. of the estate
> of Thomas Carr, dec'd. Bondsmen: Daniel M. Trammell
> and Josiah M. Carr. 31 Oct. 1853.
> p. 428. List of personal property appraised by the
> commissioners. 17 Nov. 1853.
> pp. 498-9. Petition of Louisa C. Carr, admx., to sell
> land for payment of debts. Heirs:
>> Mary Jane, wife of Daniel M. Trammell
>> Thomas J. Carr, minor
>> Louisa C. Carr, minor
>> James Madison Carr, minor
>> Letitia Caroline Carr, minor
> 24 Nov. 1853.
> p. 500. Authorized to sell land. 19 Dec. 1853.
> p. 665. Return of sale of personal property, D. M.
> Trammell, admr. 5 May 1854.

Carter, Hiram
> p. 38. Return of Seth Mabrey, admr. de bonis non,
> B. Williams was former admr.
> p. 39. Admr. files accounts and vouchers for final
> settlement and distribution among creditors, the
> estate heretofore being declared insolvent.
> 11 Oct. 1852.

Cartledge, Edmond, minor
> p. 434. Bond of Green H. Thornton as guardian of:
>> Edmond Cartledge,
> minor. Bondsmen: Rosolva D. Thornton and Robert Dill.
> 6 Dec. 1853.
> p. 636. Inventory of estate, Green H. Thornton, guardian.
> (Ward named Edward in this documen). 24 Feb. 1854.

Causey, Wiley
> p. 66. Bond of Thomas S. Smart as guardian of:
>> Joseph Causey,
> minor heir of Wiley Causey, dec'd. Bondsmen: Thomas
> C. King and James S. Causey. 4 Jan. 1853.
> p. 74. Dr. Randerson Causey asks for title deeds for
> land bought of the estate of Phillip B. Causey·* on
> 9 Jan. 1850. The purchase price was paid by D. R.
> Causey. Ordered by the court that Robert Worthington
> make title to said D. R. Causey. 10 Jan. 1853.
> p. 146. Inventory of the estate of Joseph W. Causey,
> minor, Thomas S. Smart, guardian. 9 Mar. 1853.

Cawthorn, William W.
> p. 353. Bond of Sidney A. Smith as admr. of the estate
> of William W. Cawthorn, dec'd. Bondsmen: Benjamin F.
> Smith, Stephen Cawthorn and Lewis Bowden. 26 Sept. 1853.

* ABSTRACTS OF WILLS & ESTATES IV: Estate of Phillip B. Causey.

pp. 366-71. Inventory and appraisal of the estate,
Sidney A. Smith, admr. 21 Sept. 1853.
p. 398. Petition of Sidney A. Smith, admr., to sell
perishable property. Authorized by court to sell same.
31 Oct. 1853.
p. 415. Petition of Sidney A. Smith to sell land of
the estate as the personal property, except for the
slaves, is not enough to pay debts. Heirs:

Josiah A. J. Cawthorn   Sidney F. Cawthorn
Simeon S. Cawthorn   Martha Cawthorn
William W. Cawthorn   Sarah E. Cawthorn

all minors except Josiah A. J. Cawthorn. 29 Sept. 1853.
p. 416. Charity J. Cawthorn, widow of the dec'd.,
relinquishes her dower rights in the land and consents
to a sale of same.
pp. 417-20. Authorized to sell land. 14 Nov. 1853.

Cobb, McCuin

p. 345. Will of McCuin Cobb
Wife: Harriett W. Cobb
Children: Mentioned, not named
Excrs: Harriett W. Cobb and Jesse Lee
Wit: Edwin Franklin, Z. C. Williams, James H.
    Hunter and A. P. Brandon.
Date: 11 Jan. 1853
Recorded: 11 July 1853.
p. 346. Henry D. Clayton appointed guardian ad Litem of:

Joshua A. Cobb   Nancy S. S. S. Cobb
John L. Cobb   Walton F. M. Cobb
Mary J. Cobb   Cary L. Cobb
Susan E. Cobb   Harriett W. S. Cobb
Walter S. G. Cobb   William H. C. Cobb
Jesse C. Cobb   Augustus M. C. Cobb

minor heirs of McCuin Cobb. 11 July 1853.

Cole, Noah B.

p. 333. Bond of James M. Feagin as admr. of the estate
of Noah B. Cole, late of Caddo Parish, La. Bondsmen:
Samuel Feagin and James M. Pruett. 25 July 1853.
p. 339. Appraisal of real and personal estate by the
commissioners. 10 Aug. 1853.
pp. 450-1. Petition of James M. Feagin, admr., for
sale of land for division to heirs:

Lucinda, wife of Daniel M. Dansby, non resident
Palistra L. *, wife of Edward Jacob, non resident
Manerva W., wife of Francis M. Beckman **,
              non resident
Ransom T. Cole, under age 21, residing in La.
Almira, wife of James M. Feagin
Jahazo (also Gahazo) J., wife of William Todd

*   Also listed as Patience L. Jacob.
** Also listed as Francis M. Bickham.

Mary A., wife of Federick P. Thomas
Calista A. Cole, minor, residing in Macon Co.
Amazon Cole, minor, residing in Macon Co.
10 Aug. 1853.
p. 452. Petition of Wealthy Cole, of Caddo Parish,
La., widow of Noah B. Cole, for dower. The dower is
land in Barbour County. Heirs listed the same as above
with the exception of Manerva, wife of Marvin (?)
Bickham. 4 Nov. 1853.
p. 453. James M. Feagin authorized to sell land.
p. 538. Account of sale of real estate in Barbour Co.
belonging to Noah B. Cole, late of Caddo Parish, La.
17 Jan. 1854

Coleman, Martha
p. 491. Bond of Charles D. Coleman as admr. of the
estate of Martha Coleman, dec'd. Bondsmen: Joseph R.
Coleman and Archibald Carmichael. 23 Jan. 1854.
p. 546. Appraisal of estate by commissioners.
31 Jan. 1854.
p. 547. Petition of Charles D. Coleman, admr., to sell
personal property for payment of debts, except the
slaves. Lawful heirs are the petitioners and Mary Emma
Coleman. 31 Jan. 1854.
pp. 651-3. List of personal property sold, Charles D.
Coleman, admr. 13 Mar. 1854.

Coleman, William
pp. 293-4. Annual return of William T. Coleman,
guardian of:
Benjamin F. Coleman,
minor heir of William Coleman, dec'd. 28 Apr. 1853.

Cotton, George W.
p. 122. Bond of Zodock J. Daniel as excr. of the will
of George W. Cotton. Bondsmen: E. C. Bullock and Thomas
R. Sylvester. 12 Feb. 1853.
p. 123. Will of George W. Cotton, Eufaula, Ala., and
now residing in Hartford Co., Conn.
Wife: Missouri F. Cotton, Eufaula, Ala.
Excr: Zodock J. Daniel, Esq., of Eufaula
Wit: James C. Walkley, Mary Lang and Mills Osborn.
Date: 16 Oct. 1852.
Recorded: 14 Feb. 1853.
pp. 132-3. Inventory of estate by Z. J. Daniel, admr.
24 Feb. 1853.

Crawford, Alexander P.
pp. 226-7. Inventory and appraisal of the estate of
Alexander P. Crawford *. William H. Thornton, excr.
3 May 1853.
p. 346. Cassandra A. Crawford files her dissent to the

* ABSTRACTS OF WILLS & ESTATES IV: Will of Alexr. P. Crawford.

will of her late husband, which was admitted to be
probated on 3 Dec. 1852, and claims her dower in the
lands of her husband and a portion of his personal
estate. 5 Sept. 1853.
p. 424. Petition of Cassandra Crawford, excr., to sell
personal property to pay debts of the estate. Authorized
to sell slaves. 23 Sept. 1853.

Creech, Joshua C.
pp. 430-1. Bond of Fair Pynes as admr. of the estate of
Joshua C. Creech, dec'd. 19 Nov. 1853.
p. 444. Inventory and appraisal of real estate, Fair
Pynes, admr. 8 Dec. 1853.

Daniel, James L.
pp. 14-5. Return of A. C. Mitchell, guardian of Juliett
(Julia) A. and S. C. (Samuel C.) Daniel, minor heirs of
James L. Daniel. 25 Oct. 1852.
p. 122. Bond of William A. Andrews as guardian of
Sarah Eliza Daniel, minor heir of James L. Daniel. Bondsmen: Jesse Slack and C. J. M. Andrews. 14 Feb. 1853.
pp. 589-90. Return of A. C. Mitchell. 5 Dec. 1853.
p. 591. A. C. Mitchell, guardian, files accounts for
final settlement for Samuel C. Daniel who has attained
his majority and for Juliett A. Daniel who is now the
wife of James R. Barnett. 16 Jan. 1854.
p. 662. Bond of W. A. Andrews as guardian of Sarah E.
Daniel. Bondsmen: C. J. M. Andrews and Jesse Slack.
1 Apr. 1854.

Davis, John
p. 117. Return of Mrs. Margaret Davis, guardian of:

Giles A. Davis	Capers Davis
Calvin J. Davis	Esther J. Davis
Henry M. Davis	Rebecca E. Davis

minor heirs of John Davis *, dec'd. 7 Feb. 1853.
p. 555. Return of Margaret Davis, guardian. 13 Feb. 1854.

Dickson,
Dixon, Joseph
p. 101. Elizabeth Dixon, relict of the late Joseph
Dixon **, is not satisfied with the provisions of his
will and has intention of claiming her dower and all
other rights to which she is entitled. 30 Dec. 1852.
pp. 135-7. Appraisal of estate by commissioners.
p. 138. Appraisal of slaves. 14 Feb. 1853.
pp. 351-3. Report of sale of personal property by Eli
S. Shorter, admr. 21 Sept. 1853.
p. 493. Petition of E. S. Shorter, admr., to divide
slaves to the six heirs, brothers and sisters of Joseph
Dickson, dec'd. 19 Dec. 1853.

---

*   Continued from ABSTRACTS OF WILLS & ESTATES: II, III, IV.
**   ABSTRACTS OF WILLS & ESTATES IV: Will of Joseph Dixon
     (also recorded Marlboro District, S. C.).

pp. 520-2. Petition of Eli S. Shorter for sale of land
for division to brothers and sisters, to-wit:

James W. Dixon   Alfred Dixon
William Dixon   Bryant Dixon
Susannah, wife of _____ Thally
Elizabeth, of S.C. (supposed to have married again)
          was the widow of Joseph Dixon, left no
          heirs, but claims her part of the estate
          as provided by law.

p. 523. Authorized to sell land, subject to widow's
dower. 13 Dec. 1853.
pp. 539-40. Eli S. Shorter, admr., reports sale of real
estate. 17 Jan. 1854.
pp. 572-3. Petition of Elizabeth Dixon for her dower,
which is land in Barbour County. She states she married
Joseph Dixon in S.C. and he left no children.
p. 574. Commissions to make report regarding dower
claims at the Feb. term of court. 5 Dec. 1853.

Doster, Obid C.
     pp. 577-8. Petition of Obid C. Doster to build a saw
     mill and grist mill.
     p. 579. Authorized to build mills. 9 Jan. 1854.

Dunn, E. A.
     p. 10. Petition of Edward C. Bullock, admr., that the
     sale of slaves necessary for payment of debts.
     11 Dec. 1852.
     p. 11. The admr. authorized to sell slaves.
     p. 11. Inventory and appraisal of estate. 13 Dec. 1852.
     pp. 341-4. Petition of Edward C. Bullock, admr., to
     declare the estate insolvent. 27 July 1853.
     pp. 404-7. Account current of Edward C. Bullock and
     the estate. Filing of vouchers and accounts for final
     settlement with creditors, the estate heretofore declared
     insolvent. 12 Sept. 1853.

Eidson, John
     pp. 22-3. Bond of William Broach as guardian of Francis
     Eidson, minor heir of John Eidson, dec'd. Bondsmen:
     James Shanks and Jeremiah Shanks. 13 Dec. 1852.
     pp. 54-5. Return of William Broach, guardian.
     16 Dec. 1852.
     p. 548. Return of guardian. 30 Jan. 1854.

Faison, Thomas J.
     p. 321. Final Settlement of Mrs. Nancy Faison, guardian
     of Alexander M. Faison, heir of Thomas J. Faison *. He
     has now arrived at the age of 21 years. 20 May 1853.
     p. 322. Annual settlement for James D. Faison, minor.
     20 May 1853.

*   ABSTRACTS OF WILLS & ESTATES I:. Will of Thomas J. Faison.

13

Farior, Bryant
    pp. 9-10. Final return of Seth Mabrey, admr. of the
    estate of Bryant Farrior, dec'd., with present admr.,
    Thomas S. Locke. 12 Dec. 1852.
    p. 613. Return of Thomas S. Locke, admr. 27 Mar. 1854.

Faulk, Henry, Sr.
    pp. 222-3. Heirs of the estate of Henry Faulk, Sr.
    (listed below). 25 Apr. 1853.
    pp. 281-2. Petition of A. W. and H. L. Faulk, admrs.
    for an order to sell land for division to heirs:
        A. W. Faulk
        Minor heirs of Casandra Bizzell, dec'd., who
                married Henry N. Bizzell, to-wit:
        Curtis J. Bizzell
        Henry B. Bizzell
        Jennett Bizzell
    Henry L. Faulk
    Everett Loveless, son of Nancy Loveless, a dau.
    James K. Faulk, a son over age 21
    Mark W. Faulk, a son, over age 21
    Elizabeth, wife of A. J. Miller
    E. Jane, wife of John D. Seals
    John W. Faulk, age 21
    p. 283. Petition granted . 25 Apr. 1853.
    p. 287. Partial settlement to the above heirs with the
    widow of dec'd included, but not named. 25 Apr. 1853.
    p. 315. Report of division of slaves. 11 July 1853.
    pp. 615-6. Return of sale of land. 27 Mar. 1854.

Feagin, Samuel
    pp. 127-8. Heirs of Samuel Feagin *:
        James M. Feagin, a son over age 21
        George W. Feagin, a son over age 21
        Samuel Feagin, a son over age 21
        John R. Feagin, a son over age 21, non resident
        W. J. Feagin, a son over age 21, non resident
        Henry G. Feagin, a son over age 21, non resident
        Sarah, wife of Lemuel B. Morton, a dau., non resident
        Martha, wife of Thomas C. Kendrick, a dau.
            non resident
        Louisa, wife of James M. Pruett, a dau.
        Isaac Feagin, a son
        Daniel Feagin, a son
        Nancy Feagin, a dau.
        Mary Ann Feagin, a dau.
        Mary Feagin, the widow of the dec'd.
    17 Feb. 1853.
    pp. 190-1. Final return of James M. Feagin, guardian of
    Henry G. Feagin, who has arrived at the age of 21
    years. 17 Feb. 1853.

*   ABSTRACTS OF WILLS & ESTATES III: Will of Samuel Feagin.

pp. 192-3. Return of James M. Feagin, guardian of:
    Isaac B. Feagin   Nancy Feagin
    Daniel Feagin   Mary Ann Feagin
17 Feb. 1853.
pp. 241-4. Return of James M. Feagin, excr. of the will
of Samuel Feagin. 17 Feb. 1853.
p. 245. Final settlement. The heirs are the same as
above with the exception:
    Nancy Feagin, a dau., wife of William Shipp.
17 Feb. 1853.
pp. 308-9. Final settlement of James M. Feagin, guardian
of Nancy Feagin, now the wife of William Shipp.
23 May 1853.
pp. 325-6. Return of James M. Feagin, guardian.
23 May 1853.
pp. 332-3. Account of sale of real estate. 25 July 1853

Flowers, Abner
    p. 6. Report of commissioners that the slaves of the
estate of Abner Flowers, dec'd., cannot be equally
divided without a sale of same. 15 Nov. 1852.
pp. 21-2. Bond of Harrell Flowers as guardian of Abner
Flowers, minor heir of Abner Flowers, (Sr.). Bondsmen:
Thomas S. Locke and John C. McNab. 1852.
pp. 30-2. Petition of D. A. Bush and Wright Flowers,
admrs., to sell land for equal division to heirs. (Heirs
listed in final settlement). Levin M. Flowers appointed
guardian ad Litem of minors. 21 Sept. 1852.
p. 32. Authorized land sale by the court. 21 Sept. 1852.
p. 56. Bond of Wright Flowers as guardian of Rebecca
Flowers. Bondsmen: John W. Clark and Thomas S. Locke.
24 Dec. 1852.
p. 101. Rebecca Ann Flowers selects Wright Flowers as
her guardian. 24 Dec. 1852.
p. 147. Account of sale, D. A. Bush, admr. 8 Mar. 1853.
pp. 276-8. Return of David A. Bush and Wright Flowers,
admrs. 8 Mar. 1853.
p. 279. Final settlement to heirs:
    Rebeca Flowers, widow of the dec'd.
    Wright Flowers
    Julia, wife of D. A. Bush, a dau.
    Levin M. Flowers, a son
    Harrell Flowers, a son
    William J. Flowers, a son
    Epsey (also listed as Hepsey) wife of Anthony Windham
    Jincy, wife of John Fuqua, a dau., Henry Co.
    Rebecca Flowers, minor dau.
    Abner Flowers, minor son
13 June 1853.
pp. 314-5. Report of sale of land. 12 July 1853.
p. 661. Report of sale of real estate, Wright Flowers
and David A. Bush, admrs. Authorized to make title
deeds to buyers of land. 28 Apr. 1854.

Floyd, Theophilus
>p. 229. Return of Page Floyd, guardian of Joseph Floyd, minor heir of Theophilus Floyd *, dec'd. 12 Feb. 1853.
>p. 497. Return of Page Floyd, guardian. 11 Feb. 1854.

Fowler, Enoch
>p. 47. Petition of Thomas C. Efurd, admr., to sell land to pay indebtedness of estate. Enoch Fowler left no heir within the jurisdiction of this court.
>p. 48. The only heir is one son (not named), age 21, residing in Tenn. 8 Nov. 1852.
>p. 538. Account of sale of land, Thomas C. Efurd, admr. 16 Jan. 1854.

Gamble, Ann E.
>pp. 216-7. Bond of Eli W. Starke as guardian of Martha J. Gamble, over the age of 14 years, minor heir of Ann E. Gamble. Bondsmen: Thadeus C. Owens and J. M. Starke. 25 Apr. 1853.

Glenn, Lucius B.
>p. 404. Bond of Dostheus Glenn as admr. of the estate of Lucius B. Glenn, dec'd. Bondsmen: M. M. Glenn and A. S. Gleen. 10 Nov. 1853.

Graves, Hardy
>p. 456. Bond of Stephen W. Graves as admr. of the estate of Hardy Graves, dec'd. Bondsmen: Josiah Wall and Nathan Minshew. 15 Dec. 1853.
>pp. 530-1. Inventory and appraisal of estate, S. W. Graves, admr. 26 Dec. 1853.
>p. 531. Petition of S. W. Graves to sell personal property. Heirs are:
>>Rhoda Graves
>>David P. Graves
>>Stephen W. Graves
>>John Graves, minor child of Eligah Graves, dec'd.
>>Elizabeth, wife of ____ Jackson, Pike Co.
>>Margaret, wife of Raiford Wray, believed to be living in Fla.
>>Children of James Graves, minors, names and residence unknown
>>Children of Ann Adams, dec'd., names not known except: Elizabeth, Jefferson, Caroline and Elias, resides La.
>>Children of Sarah Adams, names, residence unknown
>>Lucinda, wife of William Thompson, La.
>>Mary Miles, resides in S. C.
>p. 531. Authorized to sell land. 26 Dec. 1853
>p. 640. Return of sale of personal property. 6 Mar. 1854

* Continued from ABSTRACTS OF WILLS & ESTATES II, III, IV

Graves, Thomas P.
>pp. 489-90. Bond of Benjamin F. Foster as guardian of:
>>Mary E. Graves   Martha T. Graves
>>William L. Graves   Sarah J. Graves
>>Caroline T. Graves   Thomas P. Graves
>
>minor heirs of Thomas P. Graves, dec'd. Bondsmen:
>M. M. Glenn and George D. Conner. 19 Jan. 1854.

Greenaway,
Greenway, minors
>p. 433. Bond of Simeon J. Doster as guardian of:
>>Lucretia A. Greenaway   Leonora Greenaway
>>Jane W. Greenaway   Mary Greenaway
>
>Bondsmen: James M. Pruett and Samuel Feagin.
>28 Nov. 1853.

Griffith, Moses
>p. 77. Account current and final settlement of Seth
>Mabrey, guardian, with the present guardian, George
>W. McGinty for Moses Griffith. 8 Nov. 1852
>p. 216. Bond of George W. McGinty as guardian of Moses
>Griffith, minor heir of Moses Griffith, dec'd. Bonds-
>men: W. L. Cowan and William Abney. 2 May 1853.

Griggs, Thomas
>p. 666. Petition of Elbert Jordan and Mahala Jordan
>for her dower. She was formerly Mahala Griggs, wife
>of Thomas Griggs who left one child, Isabel Griggs.
>There never was an administration of the estate of the
>dec'd. Emanuel Evans is now in possession of the
>property. 31 Jan. 1854.
>p. 667. The sheriff authorized to summon five com-
>missioners to set dower claims.
>p. 668. Ordered by court that a writ of admeasure-
>ment of dower be stayed until ordered by Elbert and
>Mahala Jordan. 31 Jan. 1854.

Grubs,
Grubbs, Enoch
>pp. 102-3. Return of Mary Grubbs, guardian of:
>>Elizabeth Grubbs   Winny B. Grubbs
>>James M. Grubbs
>
>minor heirs of Enoch Grubs, dec'd. 11 Jan. 1853.
>p. 657. Return of Mary Grubbs, guardian. 14 Mar. 1854.

Grubs,
Grubbs, Wineford
>pp. 379-82. Final settlement of John McNair, guardian of:
>>Frances M. Grubs   James J. Grubs
>>Green J. Grubs   John T. Grubs
>>Morgan M. Grubs   William T. Grubs
>
>with Thomas S. Locke, present guardian. 12 Sept. 1853.
>p. 629. Bond of W. J. Grubbs as guardian of the above

named minors. Bondsmen: Adam Grubbs and James W. Mabrey.
3 Apr. 1854.

Hagler, Peter

    p. 102. Resignation of Charles Long as excr. of the
will of Peter Hagler *. 12 July 1852.
    p. 175. Petition of Thomas S. Locke, admr., to divide
property to heirs. 21 Mar. 1853.
    p. 175. Commissioners appointed to divide property
according to the will of Peter Hagler. 21 Mar. 1853
    p. 351. Division of personal property. 15 Sept. 1853.
    pp. 359-60. Bond of Charles Long, heir of Peter Hagler,
to refund property or money value of same provided there
are still demands against the estate. 10 Oct. 1853.
    p. 373. ibid, Jacob Hagler
    p. 374. ibid, Thomas Hagler
    pp. 454-5. Petition of Thomas S. Locke, admr., to sell
land for equal division to heirs:
        Jacob Hagler
        Thomas Hagler
        Betsey, wife of Charles Long
        Sarah Hagler, the widow of the dec'd.
    p. 456. Authorized to sell land. 27 Sept. 1853.

Hall, Henry

    p. 75 List of heirs of the estate of Henry Hall, dec'd.,
B. Williams, admr. (List given in final settlement with
the exception Martha Hall is named in this document).
21 Dec. 1852.
    p. 140. Final settlement to heirs:
    Children of W. Hall, dec'd., to-wit:
        Mary Hall
        Margaret Hall   Alexander Hall
        Emeline Hall   Eliza Hall
    Silas Hall, non resident
    Patience, wife of Charles Hall
    Milly, wife of Colly Perdue
    Daniel Hall
    Elisha Hall
    Heirs of Mary Croly, to-wit:
        Sarah Croly (or Crowley)
        Patience, wife of Jefferson Jackson
    Nancy Hall
    Dicy, wife of James Reid, non resident
    Henry Hall
    Martha Hall **
    21 Dec. 1852.

Hall, Mathew

    pp. 312-3. Petition of Mathew Hall to erect a saw mill,
grist mill and a cotton gin.
    p. 314. Authorized to build the mills. 11 July 1853

*   ABSTRACTS OF WILLS & ESTATES BOOK IV: Will of Peter Hagler.
** Not listed in final settlement.

Ham, Jesse
        p. 618. Bond of Duncan McGilary as admr. of the estate
        of Jesse Ham, dec'd. Bondsmen: Seth Mabrey and John C.
        McNab. 25 Mar. 1854.
        p. 659. Inventory and appraisal by commissioners.
        15 Apr. 1854.

Harwell, Samuel
        p. 558. Bond as admr. of Berchet Harwell (widow of the
        dec'd.) for the estate of Samuel Harwell. Bondsmen: James
        H. Harwell and James Bigham. 20 Feb. 1854.
        pp. 647-9. List of personal property, Berchet Harwell,
        admx. 6 Mar. 1854.

Herring, George
        p. 92. Petition of Polly Herring, admr., to sell land to
        pay debts of the estate. Heirs are the brothers and sisters
        of the dec'd., namely:
            Sarah, wife of John Ivy, living in Tenn.
            Nancy, wife of Charles J. Branch
            Mary J., wife of Oren Eidson
            John W. Herring
            Charity, wife of John W. Hargroves
        15 Dec. 1852
        p. 93. Bond of Polly Herring as admr. of the estate of
        George Herring. Bondsmen: West Herring and Whitfield
        Clark. 17 Jan. 1853.
        p. 148. Sale of slave and land of the estate, Polly
        Herring, admx. 8 Mar. 1853.

Herring, William
        pp. 60-1. Final return of Seth Mabrey, guardian of William
        Herring, a person of unsound mind, with the present
        guardian. 8 Nov. 1853.

Hodges, George C.
        p. 68. Heirs of George C. Hodges, dec'd., to-wit:
            Louisa W., wife of Andrew G. Neely, age 25, a dau.
            Holiday Hodges, age 22 last Apr., a son
            George D. Hodges, age 17 last Feb., a son
            Sarah J. Hodges, age 3 last Sept., a dau.
        are all of the heirs remaining in Barbour County.
        4 Jan. 1853.
        pp. 83-5. Inventory and appraisal of the estate by
        commissioners. 4 Jan. 1853.
        p. 91. Petition of Andrew G. Neely, admr., to divide
        the real and personal estate. 4 Jan. 1853.
        pp. 473-5. Petition of Andrew G. Neely, admr., to sell
        land for distribution to heirs (same as above). Holiday
        H. Hodges and Henry D. Clayton are guardians of the
        minors. Authorized to sell land. 18 Oct. 1853.
        p. 487. Bond of Elias G. Hodges as guardian of Sarah
        J. Hodges. Bondsmen: Batt Peterson and I. C. Browder.
        17 Jan. 1854.

p. 488. Bond of Elias G. Hodges as guardian of George D. Hodges. Bondsmen: A. G. Neely, John W. Bledsoe and Jesse Batts. 17 Jan. 1854.

pp. 599-603. Distribution of estate to heirs (same as above). 19 Dec. 1853.

p. 649. Return of sale of a portion of the estate, Andrew G. Neely, admr. 6 Mar. 1854.

Hodges, James B.

pp. 271-3. A. G. Neely, admr. of the estate of George C. Hodges, who in his life was guardian of:

    Elias O. Hodges

minor heir of James B. Hodges, files accounts for final settlement with the present guardian, Richard C. Hodges. 21 Feb. 1853.

Holder, Abram (Abraham)

p. 334. Bond of David Johnson as admr. of the estate of Abram Holder, dec'd. Bondsmen: John McRae, William W. Johnson and Timothy Johnson. The widow of the dec'd., Rosella Holder, was notified of this application. 17 July 1853.

pp. 336-8 Appraisal of property by commissioners. 5 Aug. 1853.

pp. 340-50. List of personal property, David Johnson admr. 15 Sept. 1853.

p. 598. Petition of David Johnson, admr., to sell two slaves that the proceeds may be applied to settle debts of the estate. 15 Dec. 1853.

p. 599. Authorized to sell slaves. 16 Jan. 1854.

pp. 636-7. Return of David Johnson, admr. 28 Feb. 1854.

Holleman, Aeson B.

p. 194. Petition of Amanda Morgan, formerly the widow of A. B. Holleman, now the wife of Thomas Morgan, for her dower which is real estate in Eufaula. Children of A. B. Holleman:

    Mary C. Holleman, minor

    Henry C. Holleman, minor

p. 195. Commissioners appointed to set dower claims.

p. 196. Report of commissioners regarding dower claims.

p. 197. Dower certificate allotted to petitioner. 5 Apr. 1853.

pp. 233-6. Supplemental inventory. 17 May 1853.

pp. 500-2. Petition of Eli C. Holleman, admr., to sell land for distribution to heirs. 9 Jan. 1854.

Holt, William

p. 347. Return of Thomas S. Holt, guardian of H. W.

(Hamilton W.) Rainey, minor heir of William Holt *.
5. Sept. 1853.
p. 529. Resignation of Asa Holt as guardian of Jane
M. Holt. 27 Dec. 1853.
pp. 583-4. Return of A. A. Holt, excr. of the estate
of William Holt for the year 1850.
pp. 586-8. Account current of the estate. 13 Feb. 1854.
p. 589. Report of sale of real estate. 13 Feb. 1854.
p. 608. Final return of Asa Holt, guardian of Jane M.
Holt, with the present guardian, Thomas S. Locke.
27 Dec. 1853.

Jackson, John
p. 557. Bond of Benjamin F. Petty as admr. of the
estate of John Jackson, dec'd. Bondsman: N. A. Petty.
20 Feb. 1854.
p. 654. Statement of account, B. F. Petty, admr.
13 Mar. 1854.
p. 654. Resignation of B. F. Petty as admr. 13 Mar. 1854.
p. 665. Bond of Benjamin F. Petty as admr. Bondsman:
Robert Dill. 5 May 1854.

Jay, W. A.
p. 449 Inventory of the property of:
John D. Jay   David Jay
Elizabeth E. Jay
minor heirs of W. A. Jay. dec'd., John P. McNair is
their guardian. 12 Dec. 1853.
pp. 684-5. Return of J. P. McNair, guardian.
31 Jan. 1854.

Johnson, James
p. 102. William Hinson, admr. of the estate of James
Johnson **, dec'd., list heirs, to-wit:
Catherine Johnson, the widow
William B. Johnson
John W. Johnson
Julian (Julia Ann) Johnson
Felix Johnson
19 Jan. 1853.
pp. 155-6. Return of William Hinson, admr. 19 Jan. 1853.
p. 157. William Hinson files accounts and vouchers
for final settlement. The heirs (named above) are the
sons and daughter of the dec'd. 19 Jan. 1853.
p. 215. Bond of Henry D. Clayton as guardian of:
William B. Johnson
Felix Johnson
Julia Johnson

*   ABSTRACTS OF WILLS & ESTATES BOOK III: Will of William Holt.
** Continued from ABSTRACTS OF WILLS & ESTATES BOOK III.

Bondsman: Whitfield Clark. 21 Apr. 1853.
p. 218. Account of sale of real estate, William Hinson, admr. 14 Mar. 1853.

Johnson, Jesse

pp. 558-9. Bond of William W. Johnson and Emanuel Johnson as admrs. of the estate of Jesse Johnson, dec'd. Bondsmen: Charles Petty, Timothy Johnson and David Johnson. 22 Feb. 1854.

Johnson,
Johnston, John

p. 426. Bond of John W. Johnston and James R. Norton as admrs. of the estate of John Johnston, dec'd. Bondsmen: Charles Petty, John W. Clark, Michael W. Blair, M. M. Watson, Arthur Crews, W. B. Crews and John W. Hall. 14 Nov. 1853.
pp. 440-1. Inventory and appraisal of real and personal property by commissioners. 28 Nov. 1853.
p. 442. Petition of James R. Norton and John W. Johnston, admrs., to sell personal property. Authorized to sell same. 2 Dec. 1853.
p. 537. Return of admrs. of the estate of John Johnston. 31 Jan. 1854.
pp. 548-50. Return of sale of perishable property. 30 Jan. 1854.
pp. 554-5. Supplementary return. 11 Feb. 1854.
pp. 594-5. Petition of Mary Johnson, relict of John Johnston, for her dower which is land in Barbour County. 6 Dec. 1853.
p. 594. List of heirs:
Mary Johnson, the widow
Margaret, wife of James R. Norton
Elizabeth, wife of William Williams, of S.C.
Celia, wife of R. E. Price
Jane, wife of Joseph Griffin, of S.C.
Patience, wife of M. M. Watson
James Johnson, residing in Miss.
John W. Johnson
George Johnson, minor
Children of Mary Ann Anderson, dec'd., to-wit:
John Anderson, minor
Mary Anderson, minor   George Anderson, minor
Samuel Anderson, minor   Russell Anderson, minor
Children of Molsey Grantham, dec'd., to-wit:
John Grantham, minor
Edward Grantham, minor
Children of Prudence Grantham, dec'd., to-wit:
Johnson Grantham, minor Mary Grantham, minor
Daniel Grantham, minor
6 Dec. 1853.
p. 596. D. M. Seals appointed guardian ad Litem of minor heirs. The sheriff authorized to summon a commission to

set off dower.
pp. 597-8. Return report of commissioners. Dower set
off and certificate filed as final. 13 Feb. 1854.

Johnston, William L.
p. 487. Bond of John W. Johnston as admr. of the estate
of William L. Johnston, dec'd. Bondsmen: Edward Ball
and Richard M. Johnston. 17 Jan. 1854.

Jones, Henry, Sr.
p. 442. Resignation of Henry Faulk, Jr. as excr. of
the Last Will and Testament of Henry Jones, Sr. *.
5 Dec. 1853.
p. 486. Bond of Elender Jones as admx. of the estate.
Bondsmen: William Farrior, J. M. Lampley, J. R. Lampley
and Isham M. Dansby. 16 Jan. 1854.
pp. 575-6. Return of Henry Faulk, Jr., excr.
p. 576. Final settlement of Henry Faulk, Jr., with
the present admx. 16 Jan. 1854.

Jones, Martha Jernigan, minor
pp. 287-8. Annual settlement of James E. Gachet, guardian,
with Martha Jernigan Jones, minor. 25 Apr. 1853.

Jones, Samuel
pp. 45-6. Will of Samuel Jones
Wife: Mentioned, not named
Children: Not named - brother Joseph Jones to be
their guardian.
Excrs: Brother, Joseph Jones and brother-in-law
Edward M. Heron
Wit: Walker Richardson, G. Toombs, Samuel Barnett
and James E. Waddy
Date: 29 July 1851
Recorded: ca Nov. 1852.
5 Nov. 1852.
p. 114. Bond of Joseph Jones as excr. of the will of
Samuel Jones. Bondsmen: James A. Jones and John F.
Comer. 10 Feb. 1853.
pp. 215-6. Bond of Joseph Jones as guardian of:
Benjamin Jones   Samuel Jones
Thomas Jones   Derril Jones
minor heirs of Samuel and Eugenia Jones, dec'd. Bondsmen: John Comer and Edward M. Heron. 27 Apr. 1853.
pp. 225-6. Glen(n)ville, Ala. Inventory of personal
property, Joseph Jones, excr. 27 Apr. 1853.
p. 663. Return of Joseph Jones, guardian of the above
named minors. Mentions slaves left to the minors in
right of their mother and under the Last Will and
Testament of their grandfather, Maj. Hart, of
Columbia, South Carolina. 3 May 1854.

* ABSTRACTS OF WILLS & ESTATES III: Will of Henry Jones, Sr.

King, Caroline E.
   pp. 289-91. Return of William L. Cowan, guardian of:
    Marshall King
    Sheppard King
   minor heirs of Caroline E. King, dec'd. Mentions
   board paid to Eli Bostick. 25 Apr. 1853.

King, Gary
   p. 65. Final return of Henry Faulk, Jr., guardian,
   with the present guardian for:
    Nancy King
    Necy S. King
   minor heirs of Gary King *. 6 Dec. 1852.
   pp. 334-5. Return of Winney Rumley, guardian of the
   above named minors. 27 July 1853.

Lamb, Jacob
   p. 6. List of sale of perishable property of the estate
   of Jacob Lamb, J. M. Lampley, admr. 12 Nov. 1852.
   pp. 81-3. Inventory of sale of personal property.
   20 Jan. 1853.
   p. 117. Return of J. M. Lampley, admr. 7 Feb. 1853.
   p. 118. Petition of John M. Lampley, admr., to divide
   slaves and land of the estate.
   p. 118. Commissioners appointed to make distribution
   of slaves and land to heirs, namely:
    Charlotte, age 45, wife of Littleton Morgan, residing
      at Ball Hill, Georgia
    Elizabeth, age 35, wife of J. F. Lacey, Villula, Ala.
    Mary, age 28, wife of L. L. Peacock, Jamestown, Ga.
    Eliza, age 21, wife of James B. Ayres. Jamestown, Ga.
    Basheba, age 47, dec'd., wife of J. B. Beck,
      Brownville, Ark.
    Malinda, age 26, wife of Uriah Moss, Hamburg, Ala.
    J. G. Lamb, age 25, Hamburg, Ala.
    William A. B. Lamb, age 24, Hamburg, Ala.
    Madison Lamb. age about 11, Hamburg, Ala.
    A. J. Lamb **.
   10 Feb. 1853.
   p. 185. Sale of slaves, J. M. Lampley, admr. 4 Apr. 1853.
   pp. 199-200. Petition of John M. Lampley, admr., to
   sell a portion of land for division to heirs. (Listed
   as above with the exception of the children of Basheba
   Beck, dec'd. She died since her father's death. The
   children are not named. 3 Mar. 1853.
   p. 200. Authorized to sell land. 3 Mar. 1853.
   p. 655. Return of J. M. Lampley, admr. 10 Apr. 1854.

Langford, Robert W.
   p. 52. Petition of Edward C. Bullock, admr., to sell
   personal property of the estate for equal division to

---

* ABSTRACTS OF WILLS & ESTATES BOOK II: Will of Gary King.
** Listed in final settlement, but not included in this document.

heirs. 16 Dec. 1852.
p. 52. Inventory of real estate. 16 Dec. 1852.
pp. 53-4. Report of commissioners on the appraisal of land in Russell County. 16 Dec. 1852.
p. 104. Edward C. Bullock, admr., petitions for an order to sell slave for division to:
    Sarah Langford, widow of dec'd.
    Frances, wife of David A. Thompson, Russell Co.
    Sarah, wife of Benjamin Covington
    Mary, wife of Jackson Averett, Russell Co.
    Edward Langford, Talbot Co., Ga.
    Robert Langford, age about 19, living with David
                  A. Thompson, Russell County.
8 Jan. 1853.
pp. 283-4. Petition for sale of land in Russell County. 17 Dec. 1852.
pp. 301-3. Petition of Francis (Frances) Harwell *, late Francis Langford, for her dower which consist of land in Russell County. Heirs listed as above with the exception:
    Edward Langford is listed as Edwin Langford
    Sarah, wife of Henry Crumpton
17 Feb. 1853.
p. 304. Petitioner granted dower. 13 June 1853.

Lee, Jesse
        p. 262. Return of George Stinson, guardian of Eliza Jane Lee, minor heir of Jesse Lee, dec'd. 16 Mar. 1853.
        p. 263. Final settlement of George Stinson, guardian, the ward is now the wife of Joseph (or Josiah?) Daniel. 9 May 1853.

Lee, Needham, Sr.
        pp. 85-6. Will of Needham Lee, Sr.
        Wife: Sally Lee
        Sons: John B. Lee
               Needham Lee, Jr.
               Lovard Lee, Jr.
        Daus: Elizabeth, wife of John W. Jackson
               Louisiana, wife of Grandbury H. Hudson
        Children by wife Sally:
               Martha Lee
               Jane Lee
               Sally Lee
               Christopher Columbus Lee
               Winefield (Winford) Lee
        Excrs: John Gill Shorter, Daniel McKenzie and
               son, Lovard Lee, Jr.
        Wit: William McCormick, Angus R. McDonald,

* The widow of Robert Langford (Sarah) is recorded as Francis (Frances) Harwell in this document.

Jesse Wilks and M. Collins.
Date: 13 Dec. 1850
Recorded: 13 Jan. 1853.
p. 86. Sarah Lee, widow of dec'd., appointed guardian of:

Martha Lee
Mary J. (Jane ?) Lee   Winford Lee
Sarah Lee   Christopher Columbus Lee

17 Jan. 1853.
p. 93. Bond of Daniel McKenzie and Lovard Lee, Jr., as excrs. of the will of Needham Lee, Sr. Bondsman: John Sloan. John Gill Shorter files his resignation as excr. 26 Jan. 1853.
pp. 110-4. Inventory and appraisal of estate. 3 Feb. 1853.
pp. 144-5. The admrs. sell surplus personal property. 3 Mar. 1853.
pp. 236-7. List of sale of personal property. 20 May 1853.
p. 660. Account of sale of cotton, D. McKenzie, admr. 24 Apr. 1854.

Locke, Richard
pp. 254-5. Account current between Jesse Locke, guardian, and Michael B. Locke, minor heir of Richard Locke. 14 Mar. 1853.

Lovitt, Joshua
p. 55. Petition of Seth Mabrey, late admr., for an order to make a title for land bought by Nancy Lovitt. (The land is in Dale County). Petition granted. 15 Dec. 1852.
pp. 62-4. Final return of Seth Mabrey with the present admr., Thomas S. Locke. 8 Nov. 1852.
p. 95. Petition of Seth Mabrey for an order to make title deed for land of the estate of Joshua Lovitt * which was sold to John Mayo. 20 Dec. 1852.
p. 377. Sale of land. 18 Oct. 1853.
pp. 614-5. Return of Thomas S. Locke, admr. 27 Mar. 1854.

Lowman, Joseph
p. 358. Bond of Mary H. Lowman as admx. of the estate of Joseph Lowman, dec'd. Bondsmen: John J. Loman and Rubin Kaigler. 13 Oct. 1853.
pp. 399-402. Inventory of estate, Mary H. Lowman, admx. 31 Sept. 1853**.
pp. 467-70. Petition of Mary H. Lowman to sell land to pay debts of the estate. Heirs are:

*   ABSTRACTS OF WILLS & ESTATES BOOK II: Will of Joshua Lovitt.
** Date given in O. C. R. BOOK.

    John David Lowman   Sarah Ann Catherine Lowman
    William George Lowman   Benjamin Joseph Lowman
    Martha Elizabeth Lowman   Samuel Anderson Lowman
    Mary Susan Lowman   Eugene Henry Lowman

all minors. John W. Clark appointed guardian ad Litem.
p. 471. Authorized to sell land. 12 Dec. 1853.
pp. 476-80. Petition of Mary H. Lowman for dower, which
is land in Barbour County. Commissioners authorized to
set off dower claims. ordered that John W. Clark, guardian,
appear at court to contest the matter of the petition
for dower. 14 Nov. 1853.
p. 492. Petition of Mary H. Lowman, admx., to sell
personal property to pay debts of the estate. Authorized
to sell same. 21 Nov. 1853.
pp. 534-5. Return of the account of sale. 9 Jan. 1854.
p. 543. Report of sale of real estate. 19 Jan. 1854.

Mann, Gilbert
      p. 659. Bond as guardian of Daniel M. Seals for Gilbert
Mann, non compos mendis. Bondsmen: Charles Petty and
H. W. Baker. 12 May 1854.

Martin, Gibson
      p. 51. Sarah E. Martin and Penelope A. Martin select
Thomas S. Locke as their guardian. 26 Dec. 1852.
      p. 52. Thomas S. Locke appointed guardian of:
          Sarah E. Martin   Mary J. Martin
          Penelope A. Martin   Seleta O. Martin
          Henry F. Martin   Martha V. Martin
26 Dec. 1852.
      p. 462. Petition of Seth Mabrey, admr. of the estate
of Gilbert Martin, to make title deeds for land bought
by Seleta W. Martin. Authorized to make same.
19 Dec. 1853.
      pp. 511-5. Return of Seth Mabrey, de bonis non, for
final settlement.
      p. 516. Heirs of Gibson Martin:
          Seleta W. Martin, the widow
          Nancy A., wife of John D. McIntosh
          Sarah E. Martin, minor dau.
          Penelope A. Martin, minor dau.
          Henry F. Martin, minor son
          Mary J. Martin, minor dau. *
          Seleta O. Martin, minor dau.
          Martha V. Martin, minor dau.
19 Dec. 1853.

Martin, James L.
      p. 58. Bond of Seth Mabrey as admr. of the estate of
James L. Martin, dec'd. Bondsmen: John G. McLendon,
M. Collins and W. G. Grubs. 27 Dec. 1852.

* Mary J. Martin not included in this document.

p. 146. Inventory of property belonging to George W. Martin, minor heir of James L. Martin, Robert E. Price, guardian. 7 Mar. 1853.
pp. 173. Final settlement for Elizabeth A. Martin, now the wife of George Watson, John F. Martin, guardian. 20 Jan. 1853.
pp. 185-6. Return of James Orr, guardian of:
    Mary A. Martin
    Victoria C. (Caroline V.?) Martin
14 Feb. 1853.
pp. 186-7. Return of Harrel F. Reaves, guardian of:
    Sarah J. Martin
    Harriet Martin
14 Feb. 1853.
p. 193. Return of William H. Martin, guardian of:
    James L. C. Martin
17 Feb. 1853.
p. 211. Return of F. M. Martin, guardian of:
    Thomas W. Martin
    Samuel M. Martin
3 Jan. 1853.
p. 427. Return of Robert E. Price, guardian of:
    George W. Martin
14 Nov. 1853.
p. 533. Return of William H. Martin, guardian of:
    James L. Martin
9. Jan. 1854.
p. 656. Return of F. M. Martin, guardian of:
    Thomas W. Martin
    Samuel M. Martin
9 Jan. 1854.
p. 679. List of heirs of James L. Martin:
    Sarah Martin, widow of dec'd.
    Mathew A. Martin, son, age 21, Autauga, Ala.
    Francis M. Martin, son, age 21, Dale County
    William H. Martin, son, age 21, Dale County
    George W. Martin, son, age 21
    Andrew J. Martin, son, age 21
    John F. Martin, son, age 21
    Elizabeth, a dau., wife of George L. Watson
    Thomas W. Martin, a son, age 16
    Sarah J. Martin, a dau. age 13
    Harriet Martin, a dau., age 11
    Samuel M. Martin, a son, age 9
    Mary A. Martin, a dau. age 7
    Caroline V. Martin, a dau., age 5
    James L. C. Martin, a son. age 3
14 Feb. 1854.
pp. 679-80. Return of Seth Mabrey, admr., and files accounts for final settlement.
pp. 681-2. Heirs listed as above. 14 Feb. 1854.

Martin, John H.
    p. 100. Return of Thomas J. Lasiter, admr. of the

estate of John H. Martin, dec'd. 26 Jan. 1853.
pp. 177-80. Sale of personal property. 23 Mar. 1853.
pp. 266-7. Return of Thomas J. Lasiter, admr.
p. 268. The admr. files accounts and vouchers and
prays the court to declare the estate insolvent.
p. 269. Court declares estate insolvent. 5 Apr. 1853.
pp. 410-12. Statement of accounts, the estate heretofore declared insolvent. 14 Nov. 1853.

McBride, John
p. 150. Account of sale of real estate, Mary A. McBride,
admr. 7 Mar. 1853.
p. 151. Return of Mary A. McBride, guardian. 7 Mar. 1853.
p. 152. Heirs of John McBride:
    Mary A. McBride, widow of dec'd.
    Catherine J. McBride, over age 21
    Rachel M., wife of William McKee, Troupe Co., Ga.
    Eliza Ann McBride, age 18
    Sarah C. McBride, age 16
    Mary A. McBride, age 14
    Sophia J. McBride, age 13
7 Mar. 1853.
pp. 204-6. Final settlement of the estate, Mary A.
McBride, admx. The heirs same as above. 7 Mar. 1853.
p. 212. Final settlement of Mary A. McBride, guardian
of Rachel M. McBride, now the wife of William McKee.
7 Mar. 1853.
pp. 212-4. Return of Mary A. McBride, guardian of:
    Eliza A. McBride   Mary Agnes McBride
    Sarah C. McBride   Sophia J. McBride.
7 Mar. 1853.
p. 574. Return of Mary A. Vining, guardian of Eliza A.
F., Mary Agnes and Sophia McBride. 13 Feb. 1854.

McBride, John, Sr.
pp. 8-9. Inventory and appraisal of the estate of John
McBride, Sr. *, by Samuel and James P. McBride, excrs.
8 Nov. 1852.
p. 89. Distribution of slaves to heirs, listed below.
24 Jan. 1853.
pp. 97-8. Petition of Samuel and James P. McBride for
division of slaves. the heirs are children and grand-
children of the dec'd.:
    Samuel McBride
    Sarah, wife of the late Jeremiah Walton
    Elizabeth, wife of Dr. Smith, living in Ga.
    James P. McBride
    Catherine, wife of Jacob Nelson, dec'd.
    Children of Jane, dec'd., who was the wife of
        Samuel Vining:

* ABSTRACTS OF WILLS & ESTATES IV: Will of John McBride.

           Jackson Vining   Anna (or Anny) Vining
           Eliza Vining   David Vining
           William Vining   Washington Vining, Ga.
           George Vining   Rachel, wife of Thomas Glover
           Sarah Vining
      18 Jan. 1853.
      p. 98. Commissioners appointed to divide slaves.
      p. 100. Return of James P. and Samuel McBride, excrs.
      18 Jan. 1853.
      pp. 163-4. ibid
      pp. 471-2. Petition for sale of real estate for the
      purpose of "caring out" provisions of the will of John
      McBride, Sr. Heirs listed as above. 20 Oct. 1853.
      p. 473. Authorized to sell land. 12 Dec. 1853.
      p. 536. Return of sale of land. 23 Jan. 1854.

McCracken, Elizabeth
      p. 437. Bond of Allen M. McCracken as guardian of
      Spencer Y. McCracken, over the age of 14 years, minor
      heir of Elizabeth McCracken, dec'd. Bondsmen: Thomas
      C. McCracken and George W. Fryer. 8 Dec. 1853.

McCrary, James
      pp. 405. Appraisal of the estate of James McCrary, dec'd.,
      by commissioners. 15 Nov. 1852.
      pp. 48-51. Return of sale of personal property, William
      King, admr. 22 Dec. 1852.
      p. 103. Report of sale of slaves, William King, admr.
      29 Jan. 1853.
      pp. 373. Return of sale of cotton. 23 Sept. 1853.
      p. 664. Return of rents collected for the estate, William
      King, admr. 3 May 1854.
      p. 671. Petition of Rebecca McCrary, widow of James
      McCrary, for dower. Heirs are:
           Alexander McCrary
           Sarah, wife of Alexander McKinny
           Francis (Frances), wife of Frederick Davis
           Thomas McCrary, minor
           Warren McCrary, minor
           James J. McCrary, minor
           Litha (Alitha) McCrary, minor
           Mary Ann McCrary, minor
      pp. 672-3. Commissioners summoned to set off dower claims.
      12 Dec. 1853.
      p. 673-4. Report of commissioners. 12 Jan. 1854.
      p. 675. Ordered by the court that certificate of
      dower be filed and recorded as final. 13 Feb. 1854.

McDonald, Alexander
      p. 348. Heirs of Alexander McDonald * :
           Mary M. C. Harper

*   ABSTRACTS OF WILLS & ESTATES II: Will of Alexander McDonald.

Sarah Jane H. Harper
Martha G. G. Harper
Robert McD. W. Harper
Ferdinand A. L. Harper
Irwin V. O. Harper
James W. Harper
Henry H. Harper
12 Sept. 1853.
p. 383. Return of John Gill Shorter, admr. de bonis non.
20 July 1853 *.

McIntyre, Daniel
pp. 23-5. Final return of Seth Mabrey, admr., with Thos.
S. Locke, the present admr. of the estate of Daniel
McIntyre. 11 Oct. 1852.
p. 613. Return of Thomas S. Locke, admr. 27 Mar. 1854.

McLean D. C. (Daniel)
pp. 72-3. Seth Mabrey files accounts and Vouchers for
final settlement with the present admr., Thomas S. Locke.
8 Nov. 1852.

McMillan,
McMillian, Daniel
p. 59. Bond of Mary McMillian and Finlay McMillian as
guardians of:
    Fairly McMillian   Edward McMillian
    John McMillian   Charles McMillian
minor heirs of Daniel McMillian, dec'd. Bondsmen:
James M. Pruett and Daniel Calaway. 4 Jan. 1853.
p. 75. Return of Finlay McMillian on the sale of cotton
and hire of slaves. 31 Dec. 1852.
p. 78. Commissioners make division of slaves among the
heirs. 10 Jan. 1853.
pp. 354-7. Petition of Finley and Mary McMillan, admrs.,
to sell land for equal division to heirs:
    Finley McMillan, full age, living in Pike Co., Ala.
    Fairly McMillan
    John McMillan
    Edward McMillan
    Charles McMillan
p. 358. Authorized to sell land. 10 Aug. 1853.
p. 529. Return of sale of land. 9 Jan. 1854.

*   O. C. R. BOOK XV, p. 542 heirs of Alexander McDonald are:
Mary M. O. Heard, wife of James L. Heard
Sarah J. H. Harper, over age 21
Martha E. G. McCarty, wife of T. M. McCarty
Robert McD. N., Ferdimand A. S., James L. W., and
William H. Harper, all under age 21, all residents of
Elbert Co., Ga.
31 July 1856.

McNeil,
McNeill, Daniel
>p. 668. Petition of Abigal McNeill, widow of Daniel
>McNeill, for her dower. Heirs are:
>>Angus McNeill
>>Sarah, wife of Hamlin Rachels
>>Anna, wife of James McGilvery
>>Catherine, wife of Samuel Whitsett
>>Roderick McNeill
>23 Jan. 1854.
>pp. 669-70. Commissioners summoned to set off dower.
>13 Feb. 1854.
>p. 671. Report of Commissioners that dower was set off.
>Ordered that dower certificate of Abigal McNeil be
>filed and allotment recorded as final. 13 Apr. 1854.

McPhail, Michael
>p. 150. Bond of Edward C. McPhail as admr. of the estate
>of Michael McPhail, dec'd. Bondsmen: Effy Williams and
>Eli C. Holleman. 14 Mar. 1853.
>pp. 158-61. Inventory and appraisal of the estate by
>commissioners, Edward McPhail, admr. 19 Mar. 1853.
>p. 174. Petition of Edward C. McPhail, admr., to sell
>land to pay debts of the estate.
>p. 175. Authorized to sell land. 19 Mar. 1853.
>pp. 229-32. Accounts of sale of personal property.
>9 May 1853.

Mitchell, P. H.
>pp. 42-3. Seth Mabrey, admr., files accounts and
>vouchers for final settlement with Thomas S. Locke,
>the present admr. 11 Oct. 1852
>p. 613. Return of Thomas S. Locke, admr. 27 Mar. 1854.

Moore, John C., minor
>p. 317. Annual settlement with John C. Moore, minor.
>John Gill Shorter, guardian. 13 May 1853.

Moore, John W.
>pp. 32-4. Petition of Jesse Locke, admr., to sell land
>belonging to:
>>William Moore   James P. Moore
>>Americus Moore   Mary E. Moore
>minor heirs of John W. Moore, dec'd.
>p. 34. Authorized to sell land. 17 Aug. 1852.
>p. 174. List of heirs, same as above, the sons and
>the daughter of the dec'd. Jesse Locke, admr. 14 Mar. 1853.
>p.222. Account of sale of land. 21 Apr. 1853.
>pp. 250-1. Account current of A. T. Dawkins, guardian
>of William B. Moore and Mary Ella Moore. 14 Mar. 1853.
>pp. 251-3. Account current of Jesse Locke, guardian of
>James P. Moore and Americus Moore. 14 Mar. 1853.
>pp. 253-4. Return of Jesse Locke, admr. 14 March. 1853

p. 542. Return of the sale of real estate, Jesse Locke, admr. 17 Jan. 1854.

Nelson, Jacob B.
pp. 28-30. Petition of Eli S. Shorter to sell land of the estate of Jacob B. Nelson, dec'd. The personal estate is insufficient to pay debts and the estate has heretofore been declared insolvent. The children of the dec'd. are:

Elizabeth Nelson   John Gill Nelson
James S. Nelson   Jacob Nelson

all minors. H. M. Tompkins is guardian ad Litem.
p. 30. Authorized to sell land. 11 Oct. 1852.
p. 109. Sale of real estate, Eli S. Shorter, admr.
3 Feb. 1853.

Norton, William V.
pp. 34-5. Petition of Isabella Norton, widow of dec'd., and James R. Norton, admrs. for her dower which is land in Barbour County. Children are:

Elizabeth C., age 19, wife of Daniel B. Snead
Amanda D. Norton, age 18
Delila A. Norton *
Nancy A. Norton, age 15
Franklin W. Norton, age 9
Thomas C. Norton, age 7
Tolbert W. M.Norton, age 6
Erban W. Norton, age 4

11 Oct. 1852.
pp. 36-8. Petitioner allotted dower. 13 Nov. 1852.
p. 149. Bond of James R. Norton as guardian of:

Delila A. Norton   Thomas C. Norton
Nancy A. Norton   Tolbert M. Norton
Franklin W. Norton   Erban W. Norton

minor heirs. Bondsman: John H. Miller. 7 Mar. 1853.
p. 174. List of heirs, same as above with the exception Isabella Norton the widow of dec'd. is listed, also Delila A. Norton. Elizabeth C., wife of Daniel Snead is listed as Caroline C. Snead. 14 Mar. 1853.
pp. 246-8. Return of James R. and Isabella Norton. 14 Mar. 1853.
p. 249. Partial settlement to heirs, the same as above with the exception of: Lucinda K. Norton, dec'd. 14 Mar. 1853.

Ochtertoni, David
pp. 43-4. Seth Mabrey, admr., files accounts and vouchers for final settlement with Thomas S. Locke, the present admr. 11 Oct. 1852.
p. 612. Return of Thomas S. Locke, admr. 27 Mar. 1854

* Delila A. Norton not included in this document.

Oliver, Milbra

    p. 452. Bond of McDonald Oliver as admr. of the estate
of Milbra Oliver, dec'd. Bondsmen: John L. Roberts,
F. E. Baker, Thomas S. Smart and John Crew.
28 Nov. 1853.
    pp. 532-3. Petition of M. D. Oliver to divide slaves.
The heirs are:
        William Oliver, residing in La.
        M. D. Oliver
        Sarah, wife of John L. Roberts
        Jasper Oliver, minor
        Henry Y. Oliver, minor
        A. Browder Oliver, minor
    9 Jan. 1854.

Oliver, Wiley

    p. 237. Bond of Milbra Oliver and McDonald Oliver as
admrs. of the estate of Wiley Oliver, dec'd. Bondsmen:
Franklin E. Baker, Benjamin F. Pearson, John C. P.
Keneymore, Clinton R. Persons and A. H. King.
20 May 1853.
    pp. 298-301. Inventory and appraisal of real and personal
property by commissioners. 13 June 1853.
    p. 335. Heirs of Wiley Oliver, who died on 29 Apr. 1853:
        Milbery (Milbra), widow of dec'd.
        McDonald Oliver, over age 21
        William Oliver, over age 21, residing Minden,
                    Claiborn Parish, La.
        Sarah, wife of John L. Roberts
        Jasper N. Oliver, minor
        Henry Y. Oliver, minor
        Alexander B. Oliver, minor
    27 July 1853.
    p. 370. Petition of admrs. to sell perishable property.
24 Oct. 1853.
    pp. 462-4. Petition of McDonald and Milbra M. Oliver,
admrs., for distribution of property to heirs (same as
above). H. M. Tompkins appointed guardian ad Litem of
minors. 11 Oct. 1853.
    p. 465. Authorized to sell land. 11 Oct. 1853.
    p. 489. Bond of McDonald Oliver as guardian of the
above minor heirs. Bondsmen: B. F. Pearson, F. E. Baker
and James M. Feagin. 17 Jan. 1854.
    p. 493. Petition of M. D. Oliver, admr., to divide
property to the above heirs with the exception of
Milbra Oliver, now dec'd. 19 Dec. 1853.
    pp. 623-8. Report of sale of perishable property and
real estate. 22 Feb. 1854.

Peake, Virginia, minor

    p. 232. Annual settlement of J. D. Johns(t)on, guardian
of Virginia Peake, minor heir of John H. Peake *.
10 May 1853.

*   From Sylvester Family History: John H. Peake was the first
    husband of Mary Sylvester, J. D. Johnston was her second
    husband.

Phillips, H. H. (Henry)
>   pp. 166-7. Annual return of Caroline S. Phillips, guardian of N. E. K. Phillips, minor heir of H. H. Phillips. 21 Jan. 1853.

Rawls, Kelly
>   pp. 206-7. Annual return of B. F. Foster, guardian of:
>>   Sally A. Rawls
>>   Kelly Rawls
>   minor heirs of Kelly Rawls, dec'd. 7 Feb. 1853.

Reid, John
>   p. 128. Petition of Jane Reid, widow of John Reid, for her dower which is land in Barbour Co. Heirs are:
>>   Margaret A., wife of William Sapp
>>   James Hugh Reid
>>   Sophie T. Reid, minor
>>   Thomas D. Reid, minor
>>   Turzah C. Reid, minor
>>   Josiah W. Reid, minor
>   p. 129. Henry D. Clayton appointed guardian ad Litem of minors. 30 Dec. 1852.
>   p. 130. Commissioners appointed to set off dower claims. 10 Jan. 1853.
>   pp. 131-2. Dower allotted to petitioner. 14 Feb. 1853.
>   pp. 141-2. List of heirs, same as above with the exception Jane Reid, widow of the dec'd. is listed. 14 Feb. 1853.
>   p. 142. Sale of perishable property, James G. Tison, admr. 14 Feb. 1853.
>   pp. 187-90. Annual settlement of estate, James G. Tison, admr. 14 Feb. 1853.
>   p. 427. Report of commissioners that they are unable to make equal division of slaves as there are but two slaves. 14 Nov. 1853.
>   pp. 466-7. Petition of James G. Tison, admr., to sell land for equal distribution to heirs. Heirs same as above with the exception of:
>>   Margaret Ann, wife of William Sapp.
>   10 Oct. 1853.
>   p. 468. Authorized to sell land. 12 Dec. 1853.
>   p. 527. Petition of James G. Tison, admr., to make division of slaves. Commissioners authorized to divide same. 10 Oct. 1853.
>   p. 631. Return of sale of real estate. 21 Feb. 1854.
>   p. 632. List of heirs, same as above. 21 Feb. 1854.
>   p. 663. Return of sale of land, James G. Tison, admr. 3 May 1854.

Richardson, William N.
>   p. 438. Bond of Walker Richardson as admr. of the estate of William N. Richardson, dec'd. Bondsmen: James W. Richardson, George H. Thompson, Louisa H. Thompson, Lewis L. Cato and G. Tombs. 2 Dec. 1853.

p. 539. Petition of Walker Richardson, admr., to sell perishable property. 17 Jan. 1854.

Rist, Calvin

p. 246. Return of Charles Petty, admr. of the estate of Calvin Rist. 14 Mar. 1853.

Roberts, William N.

p. 459. Return of John L. Roberts, guardian of:
F. P. Roberts, minor
20 Dec. 1853.
p. 460. ibid, Thomas H. Roberts
p. 460. Final Settlement of John L. Roberts, guardian, with Roberta Roberts, now the wife of Bass Nichols. The above named heirs are the children of William N. Roberts *. 20 Dec. 1853.

Rouse, Henry

pp. 152-3. Annual return of Henry D. Clayton, guardian of Mary Rouse and Ann H. Rouse, minor heirs of Henry Rouse, dec'd. **. 3 Feb. 1853.

Rumley, Elisha

p. 348. Petition of Thomas S. Locke, admr., to sell perishable property of the estate of Elisha Rumley to pay debts.
p. 349. Authorized by court to sell personal property. 14 Sept. 1853.

Russell, R. R. (Richard)

p. 73. Petition of A. T. Spence, admr., to make a title deed for land bought by Thomas A. Hightower from the estate of Richard R. Russell, dec'd. 10 Jan. 1853.
p. 123. Bond of Joseph C. Russell as guardian of:
William C. K. Russell   Joseph R. Russell
Washington H. Russell *** Lucius A. Russell
Ellen S. Russell   James H. Russell
17 Feb. 1853.
p. 218. Report of sale of land, A. T. Spence, admr. 24 Mar. 1853.
p. 219. List of heirs, same as above with the exception of the widow of Richard R. Russell, Usley (or Ursuly) and Hartwell S. (W.?) Russell are named. 24 Mar. 1853.
p. 221. Inventory of goods, chattel rights and· credits of the above named minors. 12 Apr. 1853.
pp. 264-5. Return of A. T. Spence, admr. 24 Mar. 1853.
p. 266. Final settlement of A. T. Spence, admr., with the above named heirs. 9 May 1853.

*   See O.C.R. BOOK IV.
**   See O.C.R. BOOKS I, II, III, and IV.
*** Also listed as Hartwell W. Russell.

p. 336. Return of Joseph C. Russell, guardian of the minor heirs. 5 Aug. 1853.
p. 638. Return of guardian of minors. 28 Feb. 1854.

Sauls, John

p. 67. Bond of Elijah Padget as guardian of John Sauls, minor heir of John Sauls, (Sr.), dec'd. Bondsmen: Felix Hight, Robert N. Lowe, Norman Stewart and George R. Scroggins. 8 Jan. 1853.
p. 553. Annual return of Elijah Padget, guardian. 9 Feb. 1854.

Shipman, James

p. 338. Bond of James L. and Alexander Shipman as admrs. of the estate of James Shipman, dec'd. Bondsmen: Daniel McKenzie, Martin D. Martin and Miles McInnis. 10 Aug. 1853.
pp. 360-3. Appraisal of estate, James Shipman, admr. 21 Sept. 1853.
p. 364. Petition of James Shipman to sell perishable property. 22 Sept. 1853.
p. 372. Inventory and appraisal of land in Pike County by commissioners. 18 Oct. 1853.
pp. 407-9. Account of sale of personal property. 14 Nov. 1853.
pp. 559-60. Petition of Elizabeth Shipman, widow of James Shipman, for dower which is land lying in Barbour and Pike Counties. The heirs are children of the dec'd.
 Catherine A., wife of Jonathan R. Lampley
 Alexander Shipman
 Apaline, wife of Benjamin Lampley, Pike Co.
 James L. Shipman
 Eliza Shipman
 Lucy, wife of Harvey A. McRae
 George L. Shipman
 Lewis Shipman
 Jesse Shipman, minor
 Benjamin F. Shipman, minor
p. 558. Henry D. Clayton appointed guardian ad Litem of minors. 14 Nov. 1853.
pp. 561-2. Commissioners summoned to allot and set off dower claims. 14 Dec. 1853.
p. 563. Dower allotted to the petitioner. 24 Dec. 1853.
pp. 632-3. Petition of Alexander and James L. Shipman for division of slaves. Heirs listed as above. 21 Feb. 1854.

Short, William

pp. 181-2. Inventory and appraisal of the estate of William Short, dec'd. C. F. Gerke, admr. 1 Aprl 1853.

Shorter, Reubin C.

pp. 503-9. Will of Reubin C. Shorter, Eufaula, Ala.

Wife: Mary B. Shorter
Sons: John Gill Shorter
Eli S. Shorter
Reubin C. Shorter
Henry R. Shorter
Daus: Sarah E. Hunter
Martha G. Macklrory
Mary B. Thornton
Sophia H. Shorter
Laura M. Shorter
Gr-son: Reubin F. C. Kolb
Excrs: Mary B. Shorter, John Gill Shorter, Eli S.
Shorter, Reubin C. Shorter and Henry R. Shorter.
Wit: Thomas Cargile, Cullen J. Pope, Ransom Godwin
and Selden S. Walkly.
Date: 17 Jan. 1849
Recorded: 9 Jan. 1854.
Recorded: 10 Jan. 1854 in Randolph Co., Ga.
pp. 553-4. Resignation of Mary B., John Gill and Shorter
in favor of Eli S. Shorter. 11 Feb. 1854.
pp. 641-7. Appraisal of the estate. 6 Mar. 1854.

Sinquefield, Asa
p. 545. Bond of Moses Sinquefield as admr. of the
estate of Asa Sinquefield, dec'd. Bondsmen: Martin H.
Joyce and Ransom Godwin. 30 Jan. 1854.
p. 617. Bond of A. L. Gaston as admr. of the estate of
Asa Sinquefield. Bondsmen: Ransom Godwin and Richard
Norris. 25 Mar. 1854.
p. 653. Resignation of Moses Sinquefield as admr. of
his father's estate. 13 Mar. 1854.

Slack, minors
pp. 639-41. Petition of Mary Slack as guardian of
Jesse Slack, age about 19
Francis Slack, age about 14
John Slack, age about 5
are heirs of the estate of James Lindsey, dec'd.,
of Wilks Co., Ga. Said children are minors of the
petitioner, and resides in Barbour County. Bond of Mary
Slack as guardian. Bondsmen: Z. J. Daniel, James Slack,
George Reynolds, Willis White and Henry Lawhorn.
3 Mar. 1854.

Smith, William T.
pp. 208-9. Final return of Buckner Williams, guardian
of Sarah A. Smith, heir of William T. Smith, dec'd. She
is now the wife of Thomas P. Marshall. 24 Jan. 1853.

Spear, David
p. 144. Return of William Blair, guardian of William
Spear, minor heir of Sarah Kent *, dec'd. 3 Mar. 1853.

*   Continued from ABSTRACTS OF WILLS & ESTATES BOOK IV.

pp. 203-4. Annual settlement of William Blair, guardian.
3 Mar. 1853.
pp. 457-9. Return of Seth Mabrey, admr., for final
settlement of the estate. Heirs:
    Seleta W. Martin, a dau.
    Henry G. Spear, a son
    Willis M. Spear, a son
    William Spear, minor son, William Blair is guardian
    Kitsy A., a dau., wife of John Pyles
    Frances A., a dau., wife of Joseph Saunders
    Harriet Spear, minor dau.
    Heirs of Gibson Martin, dec'd.
    David Spear, a son
    Nancy A., a dau., wife of Sion Creech
8 Nov. 1852.
pp. 461-2. Return of sale of land of the estate to
Seleta W. Martin. 3 Nov. 1852. Admr. authorized to
make title deed for land. 19 Dec. 1853.
pp. 682-3. Final return of Seth Mabrey, guardian of
Harriet Spear, now the wife of Wiley Baggett of La.
23 Jan. 1854.

Stembridge, Henry R. M.
    p. 94. Return of Samuel McBride, guardian of:
        John A. Stembridge
        Sarah E. Stembridge
minor heirs of Henry R. M. Stembridge,   late of
Crawford County, Georgia. 24 Jan. 1853.
pp. 209-11. Return of Samuel McBride, guardian.
24 Jan. 1853.
p. 603. Petition of Samuel McBride, guardian, to sell
slave. 14 Dec. 1853.
pp. 604-5. Authorized to sell slave. 13 Feb. 1854.
p. 660. Account of sale of a slave. 15 Apr. 1854.

Stephens, James F.
    p. 482. Bond of Green Stephens as admr. of the estate
of James F. Stephens, dec'd. Bondsmen: Thomas A. Hightower and William D. Hill. 6 Jan. 1854.
p. 496. Inventory and appraisal of estate by the
commissions. 23 Jan. 1854.
p. 545. Petition of Green Stephens to sell personal
property of the estate for payment of debts. Heirs are:
        Eliza M. E., wife of M. R. Hill
        Nancy A. Stephens
        Peletia G. Stephens
        Epsey D. Stephens
        Sarah Elizabeth Stephens
        Isabel C. Stephens
all minors except Eliza M. E. Hill. Authorized to sell
property. 23 Jan. 1854.

Stovall, George W.
>p. 117. Return of Thomas J. Roquemore, guardian of:
>>Cicero Stovall
>>George (W.) Stovall
>>Mary Stovall
>
>minor heirs of George W. Stovall *, dec'd. 7 Feb. 1853.
>pp. 200-2. Return of Thomas J. Roquemore, guardian.
>7 Feb. 1853.
>p. 223. Return to sale of real estate. 2 May 1853.
>pp. 687-8. Return of Thomas J. Roquemore, guardian.
>9 Jan. 1854.

Stringer, James A.
>p. 490. Bond of Jesse Batts as admr. of the estate of
>James A. Stringer, dec'd. Bondsman: W. Cowart. Sarah
>Stringer, widow of the dec'd., has been duly notified
>of this application. 20 Jan. 1854.
>pp. 550-2. Inventory and appraisal of estate.
>9 Feb. 1854.
>p. 664. Return of sale of cotton crop, Jesse Batts,
>admr. 3 May 1854.

Tate, Zacheriah
>p. 350. Bond of John Paramore as admr. of the estate
>of Zacheriah Tate, dec'd. Bondsmen: Young Smith and
>Hastin Garland. Cynthia Tate, widow of the dec'd., has
>been notified of this application. 15 Sept. 1853.
>p. 378. Inventory and appraisal of personal property.
>29 Sept. 1853.
>p. 432. Bond of John Paramore as admr. Bondsmen: Daniel
>A. Norton and Thomas S. Smart. 28 Nov. 1853.

Taylor, William S.
>pp. 40-2. Seth Mabrey, admr., files accounts and
>vouchers for final settlement and division among the
>creditors, the estate heretofore being declared
>insolvent. 11 Oct. 1852.

Thomas, Ann B.
>p. 532. Petition of Joseph C. Boylston, admr., for
>final settlement. Ann B. Thomas ** was the wife of
>Elliott Thomas who has since deceased and there are no
>living children. The heirs of Ann B. Thomas are her two
>brothers and two sisters and the heirs of Elliott Thomas,
>dec'd., to-wit:

*   Continued from: ABSTRACTS OF WILLS & ESTATES BOOK II.

**   Evidently 2nd wife of Elliott Thomas, (Sr.).

Eleanor, wife of Joseph C. Boylston
Zacheriah Grephill, a brother
Wiley Grephill, a brother
Margaret Grephill, a sister
Last three named heirs when last heard from were
     in South Carolina.
James E. Thomas
Sarah J., (Thomas) wife of (Chesnut) Faulkner
William B. Thomas
Joseph Thomas, minor
Jonathan Thomas, minor
Aaron Thomas, minor
Elliott Thomas, minor
26 Dec. 1853.
pp. 606-7. Final settlement of Joseph C. Boylston, admr.
Heirs listed as above. The shares of Elliott Thomas, dec'd..
husband of Ann B. Thomas, are to be paid to Jonathan
Thomas, admr. of his estate. 26 Dec. 1853.

Thomas, Eli

p. 56. Bond of Jonathan Thomas as guardian of:
    Mary F. Thomas   Zachariah T. Thomas
    George H. Thomas
minor heirs of Eli Thomas. Bondsmen: C. D. Bush, Aaron
Thomas and William G. Bush. 27 Dec. 1852.
p. 182. Additional inventory of the estate by Jonathan
Thomas. 1 Apr. 1853.
p. 183. Inventory of the property of the three minors
named above. 1 Apr. 1853.
pp. 309-12. Amount of sales of perishable property,
Jonathan Thomas, admr. 11 July 1853.
pp. 563-4. Petition of Jonathan Thomas, admr., for sale
of real estate of equal divison to heirs:
    Sarah Jane Thomas, the widow of the dec'd.
    Mary F. Thomas, minor
    George H. Thomas, minor
    Zachariah T. Thomas, minor
14 Nov. 1853.
p. 565. Authorized to sell land. 26 Dec. 1853.
p. 691. Commissioners report that slaves cannot be
equally divided without a sale of same. 2 Jan. 1854.

Thomas, Elliot

pp. 26-8. Petition of Jonathan Thomas, admr., to sell
land for division to heirs:
    Joseph Thomas
    William B. Thomas
    Jonathan Thomas
    James E. Thomas
    Aaron Thomas
    Charity Thomas
    Jane Thomas, widow of son Eli Thomas
    Sarah Jane, wife of Chesnut Faulkner, Pike Co.

Children of Eli Thomas, dec'd., to-wit:
    Mary V. (F.?) Thomas, George H. Thomas and
    Z. Taylor Thomas, minors.
    Elliott Thomas, minor
H. M. Tompkins is guardian ad Litem of minors.
p. 28. Authorized to sell land. 28 Sept 1852.
p. 45. Petition of Jonathan Thomas, admr., to divide
slaves. 19 Nov. 1852.
p. 57. Bond of Jonathan Thomas as gusrdian of Elliott
Thomas. Bondsmen: C. D. Bush, Aaron Thomas and William
G. Bush. 27 Dec. 1852.
p. 102. Elliott Thomas, (Jr.) minor, selects Jonathan
Thomas as his guardian. 27 Dec. 1852.
p. 183. Inventory of the estate of Elliott Thomas, minor,
Jonathan Thomas, guardian. 1 Apr. 1853.
p. 184. Return of Jonathan Thomas, admr, 1 Apr. 1853.
pp. 407-8. Division of slaves to heirs. 13 Feb. 1854.
p. 609. Return of Jonathan Thomas, admr. 4 Jan. 1854.
p. 610. Petition for final settlement. 10 Jan. 1854.
pp. 611-2. Final settlement to heirs as listed above.
10 Jan. 1854.
p. 660. Report of sale of land, Jonathan Thomas, admr.
Authorized to make title deeds to buyers. 24 Apr. 1854.

Thompson, Robert
    pp. 154-5. Hardy Graves and his wife Rhody, formerly
    widow of Robert Thompson, admrs. of the estate of
    Robert Thompson, file accounts for final settlement.
    23 Aug. 1852.
    pp. Petition of Thomas S. Locke, admr. de bonis non,
    to sell land for equal division to heirs:
        Elizabeth, wife of John Harrelson
        William Thompson
        Thomas Thompson
        Aladen Thompson
        Enoch Thompson
        John Thompson
        Mary, wife of John Evans
        Jane, wife of James Graves
        Adam C. Thompson
        Rhoda Thompson, minor
        Robert Thompson, minor
        Sarah Thompson, minor
12 Sept. 1853.
p. 390. Authorized to sell land. 12 Sept. 1853.
p. 420. Return of Seth Mabrey, admr., for final settlement
with the present admr., Thomas S. Locke. 12 Sept. 1853.
p. 615. Return of sale of land, Thomas S. Locke, admr.
27 Mar. 1854.

Thornton, John
    p. 294. Return of W. H. Thornton, guardian of Joseph B.
    Thornton, minor heir of John Thornton. 3 May 1853.
    p. 295. ibid, Edward Q. Thornton.

Tinsley, Charles C.

  pp. 331-2. Petition of Albina Tinsley to sell a slave to pay debts of the estate. Heirs are:

Sarah Tinsley, age 19	James Tinsley, age 9
Lucy Tinsley, age 15	Charles Tinsley, age 6
Julia Tinsley, age 13	Albert Tinsley, age 4
Fanny Tinsley, age 13	Albina Tinsley, age 2

  p. 332. Authorized to sell slave. 18 June 1853.
  p. 412. Petition of A. A. Tinsley, admr., to sell land in Clayton for payment of debts. Heirs listed as above, all minors. Moses Cox appointed guardian ad Litem of minors. 28 Sept. 1853.
  pp. 412-5. Authorized to sell land. 14 Nov. 1853.
  pp. 482-4. Petition of A. A. Tinsley, widow of Charles C. Tinsley, for dower which is the house in which the dec'd. lived, and about ten acres of land in Clayton.
  pp. 483-5. Commissioners summoned to set off dower claims. 28 Sept. 1853.
  p. 486. Report of commissioners that dower was set off and allotted to the petitioner. 22 Nov. 1853.
  p. 633. Return of sale of land. 21 Feb. 1854.

Trammell, James J.

  pp. 180-2. List of heirs of James J. Trammell*, Seth Mabrey, admr.:

    Penelope N., wife of S. R. Cannon, and widow of the dec'd.
    Daniel M. Trammell, a son
    Sarah S., wife of W. L. Gary, a dau.
    Nancy, wife of John S. Bethune, a dau.
    Eliza J. Trammell, minor dau.
    John H. Trammell, minor son
    James Trammell , a son (not included in this document).
    Ann P. Trammell, minor dau.

  1 Apr. 1853.
  p. 231. Inventory of the estate of the minor heirs. 9 May 1853.
  pp. 238-40. Account current of the estate, Seth Mabrey, admr. 10 May 1853.
  p. 241. List of Heirs in final settlement same as above with the exceptions:

    Simeon R. Cannon
    William L. Gary
    James (J.) Trammell not included.

  10 May 1853.
  p. 375. Sale of land, Seth Mabrey, admr 18 Oct. 1853.
  pp. 657-8. Bond of P. N. and S. R. Cannon as guardian of minors. Bondsmen: W. L. Gary, Phillip Johnson and Jonathan Thomas. 24 Apr. 1854.
  pp. 688-9. Return of P. N. Cannon, guardian. 2 Jan. 1854

*   ABSTRACTS OF WILLS & ESTATES II: Will of James J. Trammell.

Truetlin, Gabriel E.
>pp. 221-2. Account of money received for the estate
>from hiring of slaves, John L. Cleckley, guardian of:
>
>>Mary A. Truetlin   Cornelia Truetlin
>>Sarah Truetlin   Julia Truetlin
>
>minor heirs of Gabriel E. Truetlin *, dec'd.
>13 Apr. 1853.
>p. 269. Return of John L. Cleckley, guardian of Sarah
>Truetlin.
>p. 269. ibid, Caroline Truetlin
>p. 270. ibid, Julia Truetlin
>13 Apr. 1853.
>p. 271. Henry D. Clayton appointed guardian ad Litem
>of the above named minors. 23 May 1853.
>p. 468. Bond of John L. Cleckley as admr. de bonis non
>of the estate of Gabriel E. Truetlin. Bondsmen: William
>Cox and Adison D. Cleckley. 30 Dec. 1853.
>pp. 494-5. Petition of John L. Cleckley for division
>of slaves to:
>
>>Mary Ann Truetlin
>>John F. Truetlin
>>Celista, wife of Dr. A. W. Barnett
>>Caroline, wife of Thomas Berry
>>Sarah Truetlin, minor
>>Cornelia Truetlin, minor
>>Julia Truetlin , minor
>
>Commissioners appointed to divide slaves. 30 Dec. 1853.

Turk, James L.
>p. 59. Bond of Pulaski P. Hodges as guardian of George
>W. Turk, minor heir of James L. Turk, dec'd. Bondsmen:
>Andrew G. Neely and E. G. Hodges. 4 Jan. 1853.
>p. 101. Resignation of P. P. Hodges as guardian of Lillis
>A. Turk, now the wife of John W. Bledsoe. 3 Jan. 1853.
>p. 126. Return of Pulaski P. Hodges, guardian of George
>W. Turk, minor. 4 Jan. 1853.
>p. 139. Final settlement of Pulaski P. Hodges, guardian
>of Lillis A. Turk, the wife of John W. Bledsoe.
>4 Jan. 1853.

Turman, Samuel
>pp. 291-3. Annual return of William A. Barham, guardian
>of James M. Turman, minor heir of Samuel Turman, dec'd.
>26 Apr. 1853.
>p. 448. Final settlement of William A. Barham, guardian
>of James M. Turman, he having attained his majority.
>12 Dec. 1853.

Turnage, Eliza
>p. 115. Bond of Carney Turnage as admr. of the estate
>of Eliza Turnage, dec'd. Bondsmen: David Sloan and
>A. T. Miller. 8 Feb. 1853

*   Continued from ABSTRACTS OF WILLS & ESTATES II, III, and IV.

p. 224. Inventory of the estate of Emeliza (Eliza) Turnage, Carney Turnage, admr. 28 Apr. 1853.

Turner, minors

p. 104. Return of Noel W. Turner, guardian of:
John W. Turner *
Caroline E. Turner
minors. 29 Jan. 1843.
p. 557. Return of guardian for John R. and Caroline E. Turner. 20 Feb. 1854.

Upshaw, James R.

p. 116. Maria G. Upshaw, widow of James R. Upshaw **, files dissent to claims of the will of her husband and states that she is entitled to her dower according to law. 7 Feb. 1853.
p. 223. Heirs of James R. Upshaw:
Mariah G. Upshaw, widow of the dec'd.
Eugenia Upshaw, minor daughter
3 May 1853.
p. 224. Return of sale of cotton crop, W. T. Upshaw, excr. 3 May 1853.
pp. 296-8. Account current of William T. Upshaw, excr., and the estate of James R. Upshaw. 3 May 1853.
p. 443. Petition of William T. Upshaw, excr., for the division of property to heirs. (Named as above). Commissioners appointed to divide property into two equal shares. 6 Dec. 1853.
pp. 579-85. List of property of the estate. 4 Jan. 1854.
p. 628. Bond of William T. Upshaw as guardian of Eugenia Upshaw. Bondsmen: Leroy Upshaw and James H. Holsey. 28 Feb. 1854.
p. 675. Petition of Maria G. Upshaw for her dower. 12 Dec. 1853.
p. 676. Commissioners authorized to set off Dower Claims. 28 Dec. 1853.
p. 677. Report of commissioners that dower claim has been set off. 28 Mar. 1854.
p. 678. Dower allotted to petitioner.

Vann, Isaac

p.100. Bond of Sarah Vann as guardian of Joseph L. Vann, minor heir of Isaac Vann, dec'd. Edward W. Vann was the former guardian. Bondsmen: Johnson Wellborn and John C. Bryan. 29 Jan. 1853.
p. 101. Resignation of Edward W. Vann as guardian. 29 Jan. 1853.
pp. 169-70. Final return of Edward W. Vann, former guardian, with Sarah Vann, the present guardian. 17 Jan. 1863.

* Continued from ABSTRACTS OF WILLS & ESTATES IV.
** ABSTRACTS OF WILLS & ESTATES IV: Will of James R. Upshaw.

p. 617. Bond of Sarah Vann as guardian of Joseph L.
Vann. Bondsmen: Joseph M. Vann and Henry M. Vann.
25 Mar. 1854.

Ward, Ann

pp. 79-81. Return of sale of real and personal property,
B. A. Barron, admr. 30 Dec. 1852.
p. 231. List of heirs of Ann Ward as rendered by L. D.
Ward:

Thomas E. Warren	Cenia (Lucinda) Warren
A. J. Warren	America Warren
Adeline Warren	Sarah Warren
E. K. P. Warren	Julia Ann Ward
Elvira Loveless	Lewis D. Ward

9 May 1853.

Ward, Nancy C.

p. 260. Return of Lewis D. Ward, admr. of the estate of
Nancy C. Ward, dec'd. 14 Mar. 1853.
p. 261. Final settlement to heirs:
Lewis D. Ward, husband of said Nancy C. Ward,
there being no children
Thomas E. Warren, a brother
A. J. Warren, minor brother
Adeline Warren, minor sister
E. K. P. Warren, minor sister
Elvira Loveless, minor niece
Lucinda Warren, Minor sister
America Warren, minor brother
Sarah Warren, minor sister
Julia Ann Ward, present wife of Lewis D. Ward.
14. Mar. 1853.

Warren, Burris

p. 217. Petition of Lucinda Warren excr. of the will
of Burris Warren * for a division of land to:
Cleopatra, now the wife of Thomas S. Smart
Joanna, now the wife of Duncan McCall
Georgeanna Warren, minor
Commissioners appointed to divide land. 14 Mar. 1853.
p. 255. Return of Lucinda Warren, guardian of Monroe
Warren.
p. 256. ibid, Georgeanna Warren
p. 256. ibid, Burris Warren
p. 257. ibid, Bates Warren
pp. 258-9. ibid, Joanna Warren, wife of Duncan McCall
21 Mar. 1853.
p. 260. Report of money received from the hire of
slaves of the estate. 21 Mar. 1853.
p. 370. Report of commissioners on division of land to
Cleopatra Smart, Joanna McCall and Georgeanna Warren
10 Oct. 1853.

* ABSTRACTS OF WILLS & ESTATES BOOK II: Will of Burris Warren.

p. 439. Bond of Thomas S. Smart as guardian of Monroe Warren, minor heir of Burris Warren. Bondsmen: Thomas J. Lasiter and Daniel A. Norton. 12 Dec. 1853.

p. 446. Resignation as guardian of Lucinda Warren of her son, Monroe Warren, minor, and the appointment of her son-in-law, Thomas S. Smart as his guardian. 12 Dec. 1853.

pp. 592-3. Petition of Lucinda Warren, excr., to sell land that was bequeathed to children: Cleopatra, Joanna and Georgeanna in their father's will. 6 Dec. 1853.

p. 594. Authorized to sell land. 24 Nov. 1853.

pp. 622-3. Final return of Lucinda Warren, guardian of Monroe Warren, with Thomas S. Smart, the present guardian. 31 Jan. 1854.

p. 633. Return of sale of real estate for division among Cleopatra Smart, Joanna McCall and Georgeanna Warren. 21 Feb. 1854.

p, 635. Return of Lucinda Warren, guardian of Burris, Bates and Georgeanna Warren, minors. 28 Feb. 1854.

Warren, Edward

pp. 162-3. Annual return of Thomas E. Warren, guardian of:
 Jackson L. Warren
 Adeline Warren
minor heirs of Edward Warren, dec'd. 17 Jan. 1853.

pp. 167-8. Return of Lovard Lee, Jr., guardian of:
 Elvira Loveless
 E. K. P. Warren
17 Jan. 1853.

pp. 168-9. Return of William and Nancy Loveless, guardians of:
 Milly L. Warren
 Lucinda Warren
17 Jan. 1853.

pp. 171-2. Final settlement of John W. Clark, guardian of Julia Warren, now the wife of L. D. Ward. 19 Jan. 1853.

pp. 639-40. Return of sale of land, Charles Petty, admr. Former admr., Calvin Rist, now dec'd. 25 Feb. 1854.

Warren, Thomas, Sr.

pp. 326-31. Final settlement, Joel D. Warren, admr. Heirs:
 Children of Thomas Warren, (Jr.), dec'd.:
  Rebecca, wife of William Bishop, a gr-dau.
  Susan Warren, a gr-dau.
  Thomas M. Warren, a gr-son
  Joseph M. Warren, a gr-son
  James E. Warren, a gr-son
 Nancy, wife of Francis (Franklin) Anglin, a dau.
 Mary E. Wife of Absolem F. Utsey, a dau.
 Milley, wife of John M. Lampley, a dau.
 Rebecca Warren, wife of the dec'd.

James E. Warren, a son
Joel D. Warren, a son
Grand-children:
    Giles C. Efurd
    Thomas A. Efurd
    Rebecca Efurd, wife of James L. Beasley
    Children of Martha Herring, dec'd., wife of
                    William Herring
    Richard Herring
    William Herring
    Ann Herring
    Mary Herring
30 May 1853.

Watson, Peter
p. 21. Bond of Elizabeth Watson as admx. of the estate
of Peter Watson, dec'd. Bondsmen: G. W. King and James
M. Pruett. 13 Dec. 1852.
p. 127. Return of Elizabeth Watson, guardian of:
    James Francis Watson
    Peter W. Watson
minor heirs of Peter Watson. Sworn before Gamville White,
Justice of Peace, Macon Co., Ala. 17 Feb. 1853.
pp.619-21. Final return of Elizabeth Watson, admx.
6 Jan. 1854.
p. 622. Heirs:
    Mary Ann, wife of F. M. Mosely
    Thomas J. Watson, residing in La.
    Susan Ann E., wife of John G. Gaines
    Jesse Z. Watson
    Rebecca J., wife of Hinson K. Paul
    Daniel G. Watson, residing in La.
    Nathan C. Watson
    John J. Watson
    James F. M. Watson
    Peter Watson
    Elizabeth Watson, widow of the dec'd.
20 Feb. 1854.
pp. 629-30. Petition of Elizabeth Watson, admx., to make
title deeds for land sold for the estate. 14 Feb. 1853.

Wellborn, John Carlton
p. 509. Will of John Carlton Wellborn
    Wife: Mary A. Wellborn
    Mentions co-partner, William Smitha
    Mentions child, not named
    Excr: Mary A. Wellborn
    Wit: E. Sheppard, Z. J. Daniel and M. B. Wellborn
    Date: 30 Jan. 1854
    Recorded: 13 Feb. 1854.
p. 510. Henry D. Clayton appointed guardian of:
    Carlton and Lucy Wellborn
13 Feb. 1853.

Whitehurst, Levi
>pp. 358-9. Bond of Mary B. Whitehurst as excr. of the will of Levi Whitehurst, dec'd. Bondsmen: Daniel McKenzie and Wilson Collins. 13 Oct. 1853.
>pp. 384-7. Will of Levi Whitehurst
>>Wife: Mary B. Whitehurst
>>Son: Asa Whitehurst
>>Daus: Cyntha Wood
>>>Mary Ann Whitehurst
>>Excrs: Mary B. Whitehurst and Edward Byrd
>>Wit: Henry N. Bizzell and Henry C. Bowers
>>Date: 24 May 1853
>>Recorded: 10 Oct. 1853.
>
>pp. 387-8. William S. Smith appointed guardian of Mary (Ann) Whitehurst, minor. Notice of probation of will given to:
>>Asa Whitehurst
>>James Wood and Cyntha Wood
>>William S. Smith
>
>10 Oct. 1853.
>pp. 402-3. Inventory and appraisal of personal property, Mary B. Whitehurst, admx. 3 Nov. 1853.

Wiley, Laird H.
>p. 354. Bond of James McCaleb Wiley as admr. of the estate of Laird H. Wiley, dec'd. Bondsmen: James M. Thompson, Osborn S. Johnson, Churren T. Skains and Andrew T. Lore. 10 Oct. 1853.
>pp. 390-2. Appraisal of real and personal property by commissioners. 20 Oct. 1853.
>pp. 393-4. Heirs are the brothers and sisters of the dec'd.:
>>Leroy M. Wiley, living in New York
>>Thomas H. Wiley, living in Savannah, Ga.
>>Mrs. Mary Baxter (widow), Athens, Ga.
>>Mrs. Eliza Jane Carnes (widow), Milledgeville, Ga.
>>D. J. B. Wiley, Macon, Ga.
>>Mrs. Sarah Ann Hayes (widow), Athens, Ga.
>
>p. 393. Petition of J. McCaleb Wiley, admr., for division of property to heirs.
>p. 394. Report of commissioners that equal division of property cannot be made without a sale. 22 Oct. 1853.
>p. 491. Receipts for full settlement of estate from the above named heirs. 30 Nov. 1853.

Williams, Arincey
>p. 556. Bond of William Williams, father of minors named below, as guardian of:
>>Mary A. Williams   Sarah E. Williams
>>Jane A. Williams   Louisianna Williams
>
>minor heirs of Arincey Williams, dec'd. Bondsmen: G. W. Williams and Council Bush. 10 Jan. 1854.

Williams, Austin
>p. 3. Sale of land and personal property of the estate
>of Austin Williams, dec'd., B. F. Petty, admr.
>12 Nov. 1852.
>p. 145. B. F. Petty, admr., makes return of sale of
>property. 7 Mar. 1853.
>pp. 145-6. B. F. Petty authorized to make title deed
>for land sold to Thomas T. B. Vickers. 7 Mar. 1853.

Williams, Jarret
>p. 128. Return of John E. Crews, guardian of Braddock
>Williams, minor heir of Jarret Williams *, dec'd.
>22 Feb. 1853.
>pp. 202-3. Final settlement of John E. Crews, guardian
>of Sarah Williams, dau. of Jarret Williams, now the
>wife of David Davis. 22 Feb. 1853.
>pp. 214-5. Bond of Whitfield Clark as guardian of
>William Williams (gr-son of Jarret Williams, son of
>Wiley Williams, dec'd.) Bondsmen: John W. Clark and
>James Clark. 11 Apr. 1853.
>p. 316. Final settlement of C. B. Anderson, former
>guardian, with Whitefield Clark, the present guardian
>of William Williams, minor. 9 May 1853.
>p. 574. Return of Whitfield Clark, guardian of William
>Williams. 13 Feb. 1854.
>p. 690. Final return of J. E. Crews, guardian of
>Braddock Williams, who has now attained his majority.
>2 Jan. 1854.

Williams, Owen
>p. 105. Return of Jacob Parmer, guardian of E. C.
>(Elender) Williams, minor. 10 Jan. 1853
>p. 536. Return of Jacob Parmer, guardian of E. C.
>Williams, minor heir of Owen Williams, dec'd.
>9 Jan. 1854.

Williams, minors
>p. 232. Bond of Effy Williams as guardian of:
>>Betsy Ann Williams
>>Mary C. Williams   Isabella Williams
>minors. Bondsmen: Edward C. McPhail and Eli C.
>Holleman. 17 May 1853.

Willis, Sarah A. (Ann) S.
>pp. 335-6. Bond of Abner H. King as guardian of
>Elizabeth Cadenhead, under the age of 14, minor heir
>of Sarah A. S. Willis, dec'd. Bondsmen: John T.
>Grubbs and Jefferson Buford. 2 Aug. 1853.
>p. 347. Bond of Abner King as admr. of the estate of
>Sarah Ann Willis. Bondsmen: Robert Dill and Hartwell
>Collins. 12 Sept. 1853.

* ABSTRACTS OF WILLS & ESTATES BOOK I: Will of Jarod Williams.
ABSTRACTS OF WILLS & ESTATES: III & IV - Jared, Jarret Williams.

Wood, Jesse, minor
>pp. 16-7. Return of William E. Price, guardian of Jesse Wood, minor. 25 Oct. 1852.
>p. 425. Annual return of William E. Price, guardian. 27 Sept. 1853.

O. C. R. BOOK VI

Anderson, Canady B.
>p. 104. Bond of Henry D. Clayton as admr. of the estate of Canady B. Anderson, dec'd. Bondsman: Daniel M. Seals. 12 Sept. 1854.
>pp. 264-5. Inventory and appraisal of estate by commissioners. 18 Nov. 1854.
>pp. 447-8. Return of H. D. Clayton, admr. 7 June 1855.
>p. 448. Heirs:
>>Allice Anderson, relict of dec'd.
>>Thomas Anderson, minor
>>Charles Anderson, minor
>residing in the town of Clayton. 7 June 1855.
>p. 449. H. D. Clayton, admr., files accounts for final settlement with the present admr., John W. Clark. 24 Aug. 1855.
>p. 625. Petition of John W. Clark, admr., to declare the estate insolvent.
>p. 626. Heirs listed as above. 2 Jan. 1856.
>p. 627. Court ordered estate be declared insolvent. 11 Feb. 1856.
>pp. 698-9. Return of John W. Clark, admr. 7 Mar. 1856.

Anglin, Nancy
>pp. 573-4. Inventory and appraisal of the estate of Nancy Anglin, dec'd., by commissioners, Franklin Anglin, admr. 13 Jan. 1856.
>pp. 576-7. Will of Nancy Anglin
>>Husband: Franklin Anglin
>>Children: Thomas W. Anglin
>>Andrew J. Anglin
>>Joseph Anglin
>>Ann Texas Anglin
>>Victoria Anglin
>>Excr: Not named
>>Wit: J. D. Warren and H. M. Warren
>>Date: 19 Sept. 1855
>>Recorded: 14 Jan. 1856
>p. 577. Henry D. Clayton appointed guardian ad Litem of:
>>Thomas W. Anglin
>>Joseph Anglin   Ann T. Anglin
>>Andrew J. Anglin   Victoria Anglin
>24 Dec. 1855.
>pp. 580-1. Bond of Franklin Anglin as admr. Bondsman: John M. Lampley. 14 Jan. 1856.

51

Arrington, William
        pp. 66-7. Annual return of Elisha Arrington, admr.
        Heirs listed in ABSTRACTS OF WILLS & ESTATES BOOK V.
        28 Mar. 1854.

Baker, James
        p. 26. Bond of Jacob Parmer, Jr., as guardian of:
           Lydia Baker   Winney Baker
           Margaret Baker   James Baker
        minor heirs of James Baker, dec'd. Bondsmen: W. B.
        Crews and Hampton Ryan. 22 May 1854.
        p. 35. Resignation of T. S. Locke as guardian of the
        above named minors. 22 May 1854.
        p. 341. Final settlement of Thomas S. locke, guardian,
        with the present guardian Jacob Parmer. 13 Sept. 1854.

Ballard, Erwin A.
        p. 176. Bond of William L. Ballard as admr. of the estate
        of Erwin A. Ballard, dec'd. Bondsmen: Edward C. Bullock
        and Bertram J. Hoole. 18 Nov. 1854.
        p. 265. Bond of William L. Ballard as admr. Bondsmen:
        Edward B. Young and Charles D. Lany. 21 Nov. 1854.
        p. 472. Appraisal of personal property by commissioners.
        13 Oct. 1855.

Barnett, Thomas J.
        p. 385. Return of Mary A. Barnett, admx., for minor
        children:
           Julius C. Barnett
           Mary O. Barnett   Valenia (Sarah V.) Barnett
        p. 386. Henry D. Clayton appointed guardian ad Litem of
        Julius C., Mary O., and Sarah V. Barnett. 12 Feb. 1855.
        pp. 420-1. Petition of Mary A. Barnett for dower which
        consist of real estate in Eufaula. 12 Feb. 1855.
        p. 421. Commissioners authorized to set off dower.
        11 Apr. 1855.
        p. 442. Report of commissioners that dower claims have
        been set off. The court ordered dower be allotted to
        the petitioner. 9 June 1855.
        pp. 661-2. Final return of Mary A. Barnett, admx.
        p. 663. Heirs:
           Mary A. Barnett, widow of dec'd.
           Julius C. Barnett, minor
           Thomas J. Barnett, Jr., now dec'd.
           Mary O. Barnett, minor
           Sarah V. Barnett, minor
        1 Jan. 1856.

Bass, Allen
        p. 9. Will of Allen Bass
           Wife: Mentioned, not named
           Son: Willis Bass
           Daus: Molsey Sheperd
               Mary Jane Bass

Gr-dau: Sarah Elizabeth Bass
Excr: Son, Uriah Bass
Wit: L. L. Price and Josiah Bass
Date: 17 Apr. 1854
Recorded: 15 May 1854

p. 10. Uriah Bass, excr., states that the only persons interest in the will of Allen Bass are:

John Sheperd, in right of his wife, Molsey Sheperd
Fanny Bass, widow of the dec'd.
Willis Bass, minor
Mary J. Bass, minor
Sarah E. Bass, minor

3 May 1854.

p. 37. Resignation of Uriah Bass as excr. 7 June 1854.
p. 106. Bond of John O. C. Wilkinson as admr. of the estate. Bondsmen: Hart McCall and Thomas F. Baxter. 23 Sept. 1854.
p. 210. Petition of John O. C. Wilkinson, admr., to sell personal property to pay indebtedness of estate. 9. Oct. 1854.
pp. 238-9. Return of inventory and appraisal of the estate. 9 Oct. 1854.

Bass, Aly

p. 199. Bond of Peter Tew as guardian of Everett Bass, over the age of 14, minor of Aly Bass. Bondsmen: James W. Mabrey and L. L. Pierce. 4 Dec. 1854.

Beauchamp, William

pp. 80-1. Final return of Green Beauchamp, guardian of Joseph S. Beauchamp, now of full age of 21 years. 14 Mar. 1854.
pp. 81-2. Return of Green Beauchamp, guardian of Henry W. Beauchamp, minor. 14 Mar. 1854.
p. 82. ibid, Richard K. Beauchamp
pp. 83-4. ibid, Eliza Jane Beauchamp

Bennett, James

pp. 1-2. List of personal property set apart for Mancy Bennett, widow of James Bennett. 2 Jan. 1854.
pp. 59-61. Annual settlement of Nancy Bennett, excr. 21 Feb. 1854.
p. 532. Petition of Nancy Bennett, admx., to sell slaves and household furniture for equal division to heirs:

Nancy Bennett, the widow
Nevel Bennett, residing Hall Co., Ga.
Thomas B. Bennett
Silas A. Bennett
Fanny, wife of John Owens, residing in Ga.
Sarah M., wife of Charles Floyd
Louise., wife of James Jones
Rachel J., wife of W. S. Webb
Nancy K., wife of James Flournoy
Harriet E., wife of John Robinson

James A. Bennett
Eli F. Bennett
Benjamin C. Bennett, minor
Julia Ann Bennett, minor
29 Oct. 1855.
pp. 618-20. List of personal property sold.
20 Feb. 1856.
p. 672. Annual settlement of Mrs. Nancy Bennett, Admx.
20 Feb. 1856.

Bennett, Redman
p. 414. Bond of D. M. Deals as admr. of the estate of
Redman Bennett, dec'd. Bondsman: Moses Cox. 8 June 1855.

Beverly, minors
pp. 634-5. Return of Daniel G. Beverly, guardian of:
Mary Jane Beverly   Christian N. Beverly
Ann Eliza Beverly   William Norman Beverly
D. M. Seals appointed guardian ad Litem. 14 Jan. 1856.

Bishop, William
p. 107. Return of Wesley Bishop and Council Bush, admrs.
of the estate of William Bishop. 24 June 1854.
p. 108. Final settlement to:

James B. Bishop, a son
Wesley Bishop, a son
William Bishop, a son
Dixon H. Bishop. a son
Jane, wife of M. M. Lasiter, a dau.
Rebecca, wife of Council Bush, a dau.
Emily, dec'd., wife of Ryan Bennett, a dau.
Nancy, wife of Thomas S. Lightner, a dau.
Elizabeth, wife of William Blair, a dau.
24 June 1854.

Bizzell, Bennett
pp. 31-2. Petition of W. A. Bizzell and A. W. Faulk,
admrs., to make title deeds for land purchased from
the estate. 19 June 1854.
pp. 63-6. Final settlement to heirs:
Henry N. Bizzell, a son
Harrison F. Bizzell, a son
William A. Bizzell, a son
Charlotte, wife of A. W. Faulk
Jane, wife of A. W. Faulk
Mary, wife of John B. James
Sophrona, wife of Robert James
13 Mar. 1854.

Bludworth, Peyton
pp. 506-8. Petition of Patrick Bludworth and Elizabeth
A. Bludworth, widow of the dec'd., admrs. to sell real

estate in Louisville, Barbour Co., for payment of debts.
Heirs are:
    Elizabeth A. Bludworth
    Florence Bludworth, minor
Henry D. Clayton appointed guardian ad Litem of minor
heir. Authorized to sell lots. 15 Oct. 1855.
p. 651. Return of sale of real estate, Patrick and
Elizabeth A. Bludworth, admrs. 29 Feb. 1856.

Bryan, George
    p. 194. Bond of William Head as guardian of:
        Amanda Bryan
        Eliza Ann Bryan   William N. Bryan
        Benjamin Lafayett Bryan James Bryan
minor heirs of George Bryan, dec'd. Bondsman: John C.
Bryan. 27 Nov. 1854.
p. 483. Return of sale of land, William Head, guardian.
16 Oct. 1855.

Bryan, John
    p. 34. Inventory and appraisal of the real and personal
property of John Bryan *, dec'd. William M. Bryan, admr.
19 May 1854.
pp. 247-8. Prtition of John C. and W. M. Bryan for
division of property. Heirs are:
    Mary, wife of William Cooper
    Jane, wife of James Dykes, non resident
    Elizabeth, wife of David Thomas, non resident
    Sarah Bryan, minor
    John C. Bryan, minor
    William M. Bryan
    Minor children of Tobitha, dec'd., wife of
                    William Sayres, non resident
    George Bryan
    Martha Daniel
    Gracy A., wife of Jacob Green
    Amanda, wife of Elijah Bolton, non resident
    Eliza, wife of Calvin Stephens, non resident
    Nancy, wife of Thomas Varnadore
    James Bryan
    Susan, wife of Isham Varnadore
    Green Bryan, minor
    Faithy Ann, wife of William Williamson
9 Oct. 1854.
pp. 249-50. Authorized to sell land. 27 Nov. 1854.
p. 294. Report of commissioners on division of slaves
and other personal property. 13 Nov. 1854.
pp. 360-1. Account of sales of real and personal
property, John C. Bryan, admr. 18 Jan. 1855.
p. 430. Return of Annual settlement, John C. Bryan,
admr. 27 Apr. 1855.

*   ABSTRACTS OF WILLS & ESTATES BOOK II: Will of John Bryan.

p. 431. Heirs listed same as above with exceptions:
    Martha, wife of Seaborn Daniel, non resident
    Children of George Bryan, dec'd.: Amanda, Eliza Ann,
            Benjamin, Neel and James Bryan.
27 Apr. 1855.
p. 657. Return of sale of real estate, William M. Bryan
and John C. Bryan, admrs. 6 Mar. 1856.

Bryan, Susan
    p. 171. Bond of John C. Bryan as guardian of:
        Green Lewis Bryan
    minor heir of Susan Bryan, dec'd. Bondsmen: John McLeod
    and Archibald McDonald. 17 Oct. 1854.

Bush, Charles
    pp. 295-6. Petition of Seaborn J. Dubose and Saline
    (Selina) B. Bush, excrs. of the will of Charles D. Bush,
    to sell land for the purpose of reinvestment in personal
    property. Heirs are:
        Francis (Frances) Jane Bush
        Zacheriah Bush
        Charles Dennis Bush
        Selina Bush, the widow
    p. 297. Authorized to sell land. 13 Nov. 1854.

Bush, William G.
    p. 437. Bond of Jonathan Thomas as admr. of the estate of
    William G. Bush, dec'd. Bondsmen: Moses E. Bush and J. E.
    Crews. Mary Bush, the widow of the dec'd., was duly
    notified of this application. 23 Aug. 1855.
    p. 474. Petition of Jonathan Thomas, admr., to sell
    perishable property of the estate. 15 Oct. 1855.
    pp. 474-5. Inventory and appraisal of real and personal
    property by commissioners. 15 Oct. 1855.
    pp. 547-9. Petition of Jonathan Thomas, admr., to sell
    a portion of real estate and slaves for payment of
    debts of the estate. Heirs are:
        Hilliard Herbert Bush, minor
        William M. Bush, minor
        Mary A. Bush, widow of the dec'd., consents for
    her dower land to be sold and the proceeds from the sale
    be paid to her. 5 Nov. 1855.
    p. 550. Authorized to sell land. Henry D. Clayton
    appointed guardian ad Litem of minors. 26 Nov. 1855.

Bush, Zacheriah
    pp. 110-21. Annual return of William G. Bush, guardian
    of: Ruth C., wife of Elliott Thomas
        Lucinda Bush
    24 July 1854.
    pp. 182-3. Petition of William G. Bush, admr., to
    make title deeds to purchasers of land of the estate.
    24 July 1854.
    pp. 298-9. Final return of William G. Bush, guardian

of Ruth Bush, now the wife of Elliott Thomas, Jr.
28 Dec. 1854.
p. 356. Final settlement of Seaborn J. Dubose and
Selina B. Bush, excrs. of the will of Charles D. Bush,
who in life was the guardian of Rutha (Ruth) C. Bush,
wife of Elliott Thomas. 9 Jan. 1855.
pp. 550-1. Bond of Moses E. Bush as guardian of Lucinda
Bush, minor over the age of 14 years. Bondsmen: Jonathan
Thomas and Elliott Thomas. 28 Dec. 1855.

Cadenhead, Isaac
pp. 405-6. Return of A. H. King, guardian of Ann
Elizabeth Cadenhead, minor heir of Isaac and Sarah S.
Cadenhead, dec'd. Mentions $500 cash from H. T. Crowder,
admr. of estate of James Cadenhead, dec'd. 2 Apr. 1855.

Campbell, Daniel
pp. 323-5. Paul McCall and I. H. Chambers, admrs., file
allegations of the insolvency of the estate of Daniel
Campbell and prays for an order of the court to declare
the estate insolvent. 30 Oct. 1854.
p. 326. Commissioners investigate the conditions of the
estate. Estate declared insolvent by the court.
12 Feb. 1855.
pp. 403-5. Report of commissioners on setting off land
for the family as the law requires in insolvent estates.
p. 403. Return of Paul McCall and I. H. Chambers, admrs.,
on settlement of the estate which was heretofore
declared insolvent. 14 May 1855.

Carter, Hyram
p. 213. Petition of Seth Mabrey, late admr. of the
estate of Hyram Carter (B. Williams was former admr.)
to make title deeds to purchasers of land of the estate.
Authorized to make same. 21 Oct. 1854.

Causey, Creasy
p. 488. Bond of Robert Witherington as admr. of the
estate of Creasy Causey, dec'd. Bondsmen: I. C. Browder
and A. T. Miller. 16 Oct. 1855.
p. 541. Inventory and appraisal of personal property by
commissioners, R. Witherington, admr. 15 Nov. 1855.
p. 591. Petition of Robert Witherington, admr., to
sell personal property for payment of debts and division
to heirs. 19 Oct. 1855.
p. 592. Authorized to sell property. 26 Oct. 1855.

Causey, Phillip B.
p. 460. Petition of Thomas S. Smart and Robert Witherington, admrs., to make settlement to heirs:
pp. 462-4. Heirs in final settlement:
    Cullen Causey, a brother
    Greenberry Causey, a brother, residing in N. C.

Mary A. S. Barnes
Children of Rachael Edwards, dec'd., a sister
   W. E. Edwards, N. C.
   Nathan B. Edwards, N. C.
Mary, wife of Eaton Phillips
Sarah, wife of Lewis Dew
Children of William Causey, dec'd.
Children of Lewellen Causey, dec'd., a brother
Child of Polly Ricks, dec'd., a sister
   John C. Ricks, residing in New Orleans, La.
Randerson Causey
James L. Causey
Joseph Causey
Children of Eliza Turnage, dec'd.
Children of Wiley Causey, dec'd., a brother
2 Apr. 1855.
pp. 496-7. James L., Joseph W., and Randerson Causey and
the heirs of Eliza Turnage, dec'd., collected $884.77
from the estate of Phillip Causey. They gave bond to
Robert Witherington, admr., to repay as much as may be
needed to settle the debts of said estate. 9 Nov. 1855.

Cawthorn, William W.
pp. 138-42. Return of Sidney A. Smith, admr., of the
sale of personal and real property. 24 July 1854.
p. 291. Return of sale of land. 15 Dec. 1854.
p. 327. Petition of Sidney A. Smith, admr., to divide
slaves among heirs:
   Charity G. Cawthorn, relict of dec'd.
   Joseph A. J. Cawthorn, over age 21
   Simon Cawthorn, minor
   William Cawthorn, minor
   Martha Cawthorn, minor
   Sarah Elizabeth Cawthorn, minor
Commissioners authorized to divide slaves. 19 Oct. 1854.
p. 327. Report of commissioners of partial division of
slaves and the balance cannot be equally divided.
13 Dec. 1854.
p. 527. Bond of Sidney A. Smith as guardian of William
W. Cawthorn, over the age of 14 years. Bondsmen: Browder
Hays and William Wood. 12 Dec. 1855.
p. 527. ibid, Sarah E. Cawthorn
p. 528. ibid, Martha Cawthorn
p. 529. ibid, Simon Cawthorn
12 Dec. 1855.
pp. 602-5. Account current of Dr. Sidney A. Smith with
the estate from Dec. 1853 to Jan. 1855. 12 Dec. 1855.
p. 605. List of heirs as given above with the exception
of: Mrs. Charity G. Cawthorn, the widow, a resident of
Henry County, Ala. 12 Dec. 1855
pp. 606-8. Final settlement to heirs, same as above.
Mrs. Charity G. Cawthorn's share included money from
sale of dower lands. 28 Jan. 1856.

Chaney,
Chany, John
>p. 434. Bond of John Helms as admr. of the estate of
John Chany, dec'd. Bondsmen: John C. McNab and Seth
Mabrey. 22 June 1855.
>pp. 586- 8. Final settlement of John Helms with the
two heirs:
>>Milbry Chaney, widow of dec'd.
Holly Helms, wife of John Helms, a dau. of dec'd.
>1 Oct. 1855.

Claybrook, Robert W.
>p. 175. Bond as admr. of Benjamin Screws for the estate
of Robert W. Claybrook, dec'd. Bondsmen: W. L. Keneday
and James E. Barnett. 8 Nov. 1854.
>pp. 266-7. Schedule of effects of the estate appraised
by commissioners. 24 Nov. 1854.
>p. 269. Petition of Benjamin Screws for sale of personal
property. 24 Nov. 1854.

Cobb, McCuin
>p. 530. Inventory and apprasal of personal property
by commissioners, J. W. Clark, admr. 8 Dec. 1855.
>p. 596. Final settlement of Thomas S. Locke with the
present admr. 8 Oct. 1855.

Cole. Edwin J.
>p. 402. Thomas S. Locke appointed admr. de bonis non of
the estate of Edwin J. Cole *. Bondsmen: Jesse B. Coleman and Charles Petty. 31 Mar. 1855.

Coleman, Martha
>p. 245. Petition of Charles D. Coleman, admr., to sell
slaves to pay debts of the estate. Heirs are:
>>Charles D. Coleman, the petitioner
Mary Emma Coleman, minor
>12 Sept. 1854.
>pp. 246-7. Authorized to sell slaves. 13 Nov. 1854.
>p. 290. Return of Charles D. Coleman, admr., on the
sale of slaves. 15 Dec. 1854.
>p. 608. Bond of Josiah Hancock as guardian of Mary
Emily (Emma?) Coleman. Bondsman: Joseph West.
>4 Feb. 1856.

Coleman, William
>pp. 76-7. Return of William T. Coleman, guardian of
Benjamin F. Coleman, minor. 6 Mar. 1854.

Cowart, William
>p. 490. Bond of Daniel M. Seals as admr. of the estate
of William Cowart, dec'd. Bondsmen: John Gill Shorter

---

* Continued from ABSTRACTS OF WILLS & ESTATES BOOKS: I, II,
III, and IV.

and H. D. Clayton. 26 Oct. 1855.
p. 505. Susan M. Cowart, widow of William Cowart *, files her dissent to his will and wants her portion of the estate she would have been entitled had he died intestate. The legatees are:

    Susan M. Cowart, the widow
    William J. Cowart
    Eliza M. Cowart
    Sophia A. Cowart

13 Nov. 1855.
p. 601. Daniel M. Seals, admr., files his suggestion of the solvency of the estate and prays for an order to set apart to Susan M. Cowart, widow of the dec'd., her portion of the personal property of the estate, she having filed her dissent to the will of her late husband. 10 Dec. 1855.
pp. 658-60. Inventory and appraisal of real and personal ptoperty by commissioners. 8 Mar. 1856.

Crawford, A. P. (Alexander)
p. 88. Petition of Cassandra A. Crawford, excr. of the will of A. P. Crawford, to sell lot in Eufaula to pay debts of the estate. Heirs are children of the dec'd.:

    Ella Roberta Crawford
    Virginia Penn Crawford
    Alexander Penn Crawford
    Virgil Crawford

26 Sept. 1853.
p. 426. Heirs listed same as above. Children are minors. C. A. Crawford, excr. 8 June 1855.

Creech, Joshua C.
pp. 113-4. Fair Pines (Pynes) admr. of the estate, states that the personal assets are insufficient to pay debts and petitions for a sale of a portion of land in Barbour and Henry Counties. 21 Feb. 1954.
p. 115. Heirs are:

    David Creech, minor
    Wesley Creech, minor
    Francis Creech, minor, residence unknown

D. M. Seals appointed guardian ad Litem of minbrs. 10 Apr. 1854.
p. 155. Return of Fair Pynes, admr., on sale of rea estate in Barbour and Henry Counties. 24 Aug. 1854.

Daniel, James L.
pp. 144-6. Annual settlement of William A. Andrews, guardian of Sarah E. Daniel, minor heir of James L. Daniel, dec'd. 3 May 1854.

*   O. C. R. BOOK VII, p. 214: Will of William Cowart.

Dickson, minor
> p. 530. Bond of John J. Dickson as guardian of Luna A.
> Dickson, minor under the age of 14 years. Bondsmen:
> Ira Britt and Eldrige Meadley (Medley?). 1 Dec. 1855.

Dixon, Joseph
> pp. 12-20. Annual return of Eli S. Shorter, admr.
> 25 Mar. 1854.
> pp. 16-17. Agreement of partnership of Joseph Dixon
> with Robert A. McTyer of Marlborough District, S. C.
> pp. 363-5. Report of commissioners on division of
> slaves. List of slaves allotted to the widow, Elizabeth
> Dixon. The balance of slaves cannot be equally divided
> without a sale of same. 6 Jan. 1854.
> pp. 493-4. Return of sale of slaves, Eli S. Shorter,
> admr. 5 Nov. 1855.
> p. 494. Annual return of Eli S. Shorter. 5 Nov. 1855.

Edge, William
> p. 36. List of inventory and appraisal of estate.
> 5 June 1854.
> p. 211. Petition of Thomas S. Locke, admr. to sell
> perishable property. Heirs are:
>> Jesse Edge   Levi Edge
>> William Edge   Jenny Edge, non resident
>> Eli Edge   widow of the dec'd.
>
> 9 Oct. 1854.
> p. 286. List of property sold, Thomas S. Locke admr.
> 11 Dec. 1854.
> p. 594. Petition of Thomas S. Locke to declare the
> estate insolvent.
> p. 595. Court ordered that the estate be declared
> insolvent and notices given to creditors. 13 June 1855.

Efurd, Giles C.
> pp. 293-4. Final return of Ira Lampley, guardian of
> Giles C. Efurd, who has arrived at the age of
> 21 years. 11 Dec. 1854.

Eidson, John
> p. 572. Final settlement of William Broach, guardian
> of Francis Eidson, who has now attained his majority.
> 7 Jan. 1856. (Heir of John Edison).

Faison, Thomas J.
> p. 33. Annual return of Nancy Faison, guardian of
> James D. Faison, minor. 3 May 1854.

Faulk, Henry, Sr.
> p. 620. Return of A. W. and H. L. Faulk, admrs.
> 5 Jan. 1856.
> pp. 621-2. Final settlement of estate to:
>> A. W. Faulk
>> Henry L. Faulk

M. W. Faulk
John W. Faulk
James K. Faulk
John D. Seals, in right of his wife, Jane
A. J. Miller, in right of his wife, Elizabeth
Everett Loveless, gr-son, in right of his mother,
           Nancy Loveless
Children of Casandra Bizzell: Henry B. Bizzell,
        James C. Bizzell and Mary J. Bizzell.
    5 Jan. 1856.

Faulk, Jesse
        p. 39. Bond of Nancy Faulk and W. J. Grubbs as admrs.
        of the estate of Jesse Faulk, dec'd. Bondsmen: D. M.
        McKenzie and James K. Turner. 24 June 1854.
        pp. 159-60. List of sale of personal property, W. J.
        Grubbs, admr. 2 Sept. 1854.
        pp. 178-80. Inventory and appraisal of personal property
        by commissioners. 24 July 1854.
        p. 186. Petition of W. J. Grubbs and Nancy Faulk to
        sell perishable property. 25 July 1854.
        p. 302. Return of W. J. Grubbs, admr. 1 Jan. 1855.
        p. 320. Petition of Nancy Faulk, widow of Jesse Faulk,
        for dower which is land situated in the town of Louis-
        ville, Barbour Co., also land known as the plantation
        of the dec'd. Children of Jesse Faulk are all minors:
            Sarah Elizabeth Faulk   Martha A. E. Faulk
            Mary L. Faulk   Isabel A. Faulk
            James E. Faulk
        p. 321. Commissioners authorized to set off dower.
        20 Nov. 1854.
        pp. 322-3. Report of commissioners that dower claims
        were set off. Ordered that the report be filed and
        dower allotted to petitioner. 15 Jan. 1855.
        p. 650. Annual return of W. J. Grubbs and Nancy Faulk,
        admrs. 29 Feb. 1856.
        p. 660. Return of Worthy J. Grubbs and Nancy Faulk.
        14 Mar. 1856.

Feagin, Samuel
        p. 132. Return of James M. Feagin, guardian of:
            Isaac B. Feagin
            Daniel Feagin
            Mary Ann Feagin
        6 June 1854.

Flake, William
        p. 576. Bond of Benjamin C. Flake as guardian of:
            Florida Flake   William Flake
            Martha Jane Flake   Eugenia V. Flake

minor heirs of William Flake *, dec'd. Bondsman:
Robert Furgeson. 15 Jan. 1856.

Flowers, Abner

p. 57. Final settlement of Harrel Flowers, guardian
of Abner Flowers, who has now attained his majority.
20 Feb. 1854.

Floyd, Theophilus

p. 629. Return of Page Floyd, guardian of Joseph Floyd
minor heir of Theophilus Floyd. 13 Feb. 1856.

Ford, Gardner

p. 173. Bond of Eli N. Ford and William G. Ford as
admrs. of the estate of Gardner Ford. dec'd. Bondsmen:
G. W. King, Levy King, W. A. Weldon and M. S. Taylor.
11 Sept. 1854.
p. 210. Petition of E. N. Ford and William G. Ford,
admrs., to sell cotton crop and divide property among
heirs:
> William G. Ford
> Eli N. Ford
> Children of James Ford, dec'd., to-wit:
> > Elcana G. Ford
> > James P. Ford

Commissioners appointed to divide real and personal
property. 9 Oct. 1854.
p. 230. Inventory of personal property by commissioners.
9 Oct. 1854.
p. 293. Commissioners report they are unable to make equal
division of property. The admrs. ordered to sell slaves
for equal division. 13 Nov. 1854.
pp. 689-91. Return of admrs. on sale of personal property.
11 Feb. 1856.

Gamble, Ann E.

p. 340. Bond of E. William Starke as admr. of the estate
of Ann E. Gamble. Bondsmen: T. C. Owens and A. B. Starke.
28 Oct. 1854.
pp. 344-5. Inventory and appraisal of personal property
by commissioners. 13 Dec. 1854.
pp. 345-6. Petition of Eli W. Starke, admr., for an
order of distribution of property to:
> Francis (Frances) C., wife of Eli W. Starke,
> > Pike County, Ala.
> Martha J. Gamble, minor dau., ward of Eli W. Starke.
15. Dec. 1854.

Gary, William L.

pp. 502-3. Inventory and appraisal of personal property
by commissioners. 12 Nov. 1855.

* Name William Flake from the 1850 Barbour County Census.

pp. 503-4. Petition of James Gary, admr., to sell
perishable property. 12 Nov. 1855.
pp. 562-4. Petition of James Gary, admr., to sell land
to settle debts of the estate. Heirs are:
    Sarah J. Gary, widow of the dec'd.
    Henry Daniel Gary, minor
    Frances L. Gary, minor
Henry D. Clayton appointed guardian ad Litem of minors.
12 Nov. 1855.
p. 565. Authorized to sell land. 24 Dec. 1855.
pp. 570-2. Return of sales of personal property, James
Gary, admr. 7 Jan. 1856.

Grantham, Molsey
    p. 699. Bond of W. B. Crews as guardian of John J.
    Grantham, minor heir of Molsey Grantham, dec'd. Bonds-
    men: James R. Norton and John E. Crews. 29 Mar. 1856.

Grantham, William
    p. 182. Bond of Thomas S. Locke as admr. of the estate
    of William Grantham, dec'd. Bondsman: D. M. Seals.
    24 July 1854.
    p. 394. Bond as guardian of D. M. Seals for:
        Martha Grantham   Jesse Grantham
        Mary Grantham   Jincy Grantham
    Bondsman: H. D. Clayton. 27 Mar. 1855.

Green, Hinchy
    p. 500. Petition of James L. Pugh, admr., to sell
    perishable property of the estate for payment of
    debts. 5 Nov. 1855.
    p. 501. Petition of James L. Pugh to divide slaves to:
        Sarah Green   Violetta Green
        Isabella Green   Mary Green
        William L. Green   Ann Green
Commissioners appointed to divide slaves. 5 Nov. 1855.
pp. 536-7. Petition of James L. Pugh, admr., to sell
land for equal division to heirs. Heirs listed as
above with the exceptions:
    Violetta Green, minor
    Mary Green, minor   Ann Green, minor ,
5 Nov. 1855.
p. 538. Authorized to sell land. 17 Dec. 1855.
pp. 600-1. Commissioners appointed to divide slaves
report that equal division cannot be made without a
sale. 13 Nov. 1855.

Griffith, Moses
    pp. 157-9. Final settlement of Mrs. Elizabeth C.
    McGinty and her husband, George W. McGinty, with Seth
    Mabrey, the present guardian of Moses Griffith.
    8 May 1854.

Grubbs, Enoch
>p. 203. Bond of Mary Grubbs as guardian of:
>>Elizabeth Grubbs
>>James Grubbs
>
>minor heirs of Enoch Grubbs. Bondsmen: John Sasser and Winney B. Grubbs. 11 Dec. 1854.
>p. 391. Final return of Mary Grubbs, guardian of Winney B. Grubbs, now of the age of 21 years, heir of Enoch Grubbs, dec'd. 12 Feb. 1855.

Hagler, Henry
>pp. 106-7. Bond of Franklin E. Baker as admr. of the estate of Henry Hagler. Bondsmen: Niecy L. Lewis and Whitfield Clark. 23 Sept. 1854.
>p. 273. Inventory and appraisal by commissioners. 2 Dec. 1854.
>p. 275. Petition of Franklin E. Baker to sell a portion of personal property for payment of debts. 5 Dec. 1854.
>p. 385. Return of sale of personal property. 21 Mar. 1855.

Hagler, Peter
>pp. 73-6. Petition of Thomas S. locke to sell land for division to heirs. 13 Mar. 1854.

Hamrick, John M.
>p. 122. Bond of John M. White as admr. of the estate of John M. Hamrick, dec'd. Bondsman: William Ivey. The widow of the said dec'd., Edy M. Hamrick has been notified of this application. 4 Nov. 1854.
>pp. 275-6. Inventory and appraisal of personal property by commissioners. 8 Dec. 1854.

Harwell, Samuel
>pp. 501-2. Petition of James H. Harwell, admr., for division of slaves to:
>>Berchet Harwell, the widow of the dec'd.
>>Samuel W. Harwell
>>James H. Harwell
>>Jesse (Jessie) Taylor, in right of her father Henry J. Harwell, Montgomery, Ala.
>>Frances L. wife of William McLeod
>>Samantha, wife of Eli C. Holleman
>>Children of Elizabeth T. Birdsong, dec'd., to-wit:
>>>Martha Ann Birdsong, minor, Tallapoosa Co., Ala.
>>>Josephine Birdsong, minor, Tallapoosa Co., Ala.
>>>William H. Birdsong, minor, Tallapoosa Co., Ala.
>>Children of Eliza Ann Gardner, dec'd., to-wit:
>>>Samuel H. Gardner, minor, Pike Co., Ala.
>>>Frances H. Gardner, minor, Pike Co., Ala.
>
>8 Nov. 1855.
>p. 559. Return of Berchet Harwell, special admx. of estate, and files accounts for final settlement. 12 Nov. 1855.

pp. 560-1. Ordered that accounts be given to James
H. Harwell, admr. 24 Dec. 1855.
p. 597. Petition of James H. Harwell, admr., to sell
a portion of personal property for payment of debts.
Heirs listed as above. 8 Nov. 1855.
p. 598. Authorized to sell property. 15 Dec. 1855.
pp. 599-600. Report of commissioners appointed to
divide slaves. 16 Nov. 1855.
pp. 623-5. Return of sales of personal property revised
by James H. Harwell, admr. 12 Feb. 1856.

Head, John M.
p. 483. Bond of William Head as admr. of estate of
John M. Head, dec'd. Bondsmen: R. T. White and Henry N.
Urquhart. 16 Oct. 1855.

Hendrix, Mary M.
p. 477. Inventory and appraisal of the personal property
by commissioners, R. C. Ethridge, admr. 18 Oct. 1855.
p. 481. Will of Mary M. Hendrix
    Daus: Sinthy Muncours
          Betsey G. Ethridge
    Micajah Allen to have five dollars.
    Excr: Richard C. Ethridge
    Date: 19 May 1851
    Recorded: 8 Oct. 1855.
p. 481. Citations to appear at court issued to:
    Sinthy Muncours, a dau.
    Micajah Allen, a gr-son, non resident
10 Sept. 1855.
p. 485. Bond of Richard C. Ethridge as excr. of the
will of Mary M. Hendrix. Bondsmen: Isaiah Smith and
Thomas W. Richards. 8 Oct. 1855.

Herring, Martha
p. 361. Bond of Giles C. Efurd as guardian of Mary Ann
Herring, minor under the age of 14 years, heir of
Martha Herring, dec'd. Bondsmen: Patrick Bludworth and
J. M. Lampley. 15 Jan. 1855.
p. 436. Bond of Giles C. Efurd as guardian of Richard
H. Herring, minor. Bondsman: S. Mabrey. 22 Aug. 1855.
p. 437. ibid, William W. Herring.

Herring, William
p. 90. Annual return of Thomas S. Locke, guardian of
William Herring, a person of unsound mind.
27 Mar. 1854.
p. 103. Bond of Buckner Williams as guardian. Bondsman: T. C. Efurd. 27 July 1854.
p. 338. Final settlement of Thomas S. Locke, guardian,
with the present guardian, Buckner Williams.
13 Sept. 1854

Hinson, William
     p. 441. Nancy Jane Hinson selects Dixon H. Bishop as her guardian. 15 Sept. 1855
     p. 442. Bond of Dixon H. Bishop as guardian of Nancy Jane Hinson, minor of the age of 14, heir of William Hinson, dec'd. Bondsmen: B.F. Streeter and S. M. Streeter. 15 Sept. 1855.

Hodges, George C.
     pp. 129-30. Petition of Andrew G. Neely, admr., to sell undivided half of personal property for distribution to heirs:
          Louisa W. Neely, wife of the petitioner
          Holiday H. Hodges
          George D. Hodges, minor
          Sarah Hodges, minor
     23 May 1854.
     p. 166. Sale of personal property, Andrew G. Neely, admr. 12 Sept. 1854.
     pp. 204-6. Return of E. G. Hodges, guardian of Sarah J. and George D. Hodges. 6 June 1854.
     pp. 251-3. Petition of Elias G. Hodges, guardian of Sarah J. Hodges, to sell real and personal property of his ward for the purpose of loaning proceeds at interest. 17 Sept. 1854.
     p. 254. Authorized to sell property. 24 Oct. 1854.
     p. 401. Return of sale of real and personal property, E. G. Hodges, guardian. 2 Apr. 1855.

Holleman, Aeson
     pp. 234-7. Petition of Eli C. Holleman to sell lots in Eufaula for equal division to heirs:
          Amanda, widow of dec'd., has since married Thomas Morgan and resides in Eufaula.
          Mary Holleman, minor
          Henry Holleman, minor
     p. 238. Authorized to sell land. 6 Oct. 1854.

Hood, Bold Robin
     pp. 284. Will of Bold Robin Hood
       Sons: Joshua T. Hood
            Daniel S. Hood
       Gr-dau: Mary Jane Hood
       Gr-sons: Daniel S. Hood, son of Daniel S. Hood
            Bold Robin Hood, son of Joshua T. Hood
       Excr: Son, Joshua T. Hood
       Wit: D. S. Cole, Elizabeth Arrington and
            T. C. Efurd.
       Date: 20 Sept. 1838
       Recorded: 12 Dec. 1854.

Hughey, James W.
     p. 443. Bond of Adam Grubbs and John A. Reynolds as

admrs. of the estate of James W. Hughey, dec'd. Bondsman: Worthy J. Grubbs. 19 Sept. 1855.
pp. 472-3. Appraisal of estate by commissioners.
15 Oct. 1855.
p. 491. Petition of Adam Grubbs and John A. Reynolds,
admrs., to sell perishable property of the estate.
25 Oct. 1855.
pp. 551-3. Return of sale of personal property, Adam
Grubbs, admr. 10 Dec. 1855.

Jay, W. A.
    p. 439. Bond of John P. McNair as guardian of John D.
Jay, minor heir of W. A. Jay. Bondsmen: H. J. Marley,
Randall McNair and John McNab. 31 Aug. 1855.
p. 440. ibid, David Jay
p. 445. Bond as guardian of John P. McNair for Elizabeth
E. Jay. 31 Aug. 1855.
p. 667. Return of John P. McNair, guardian of John D.
Jay, minor. 15 Feb. 1856.
p.667. ibid, David Jay
p. 668. ibid, Elizabeth E. Jay

Johnson, Emanuel
    p. 648. Bond of William W. Johnson as admr. of the
estate of Emanuel Johnson, dec'd., Bondsmen: David
Johnson, Clark Echols and Thomas E. McCrackin.
1 Mar. 1856.
pp. 664-5. Inventory and appraisal of the estate,
W. W. Johnson, admr. 20 Mar. 1856.

Johnson, James
    pp. 43-5. Return of Henry D. Clayton, guardian of:
        William B. Johnson
        Felix Johnson
        Julia Johnson   (All heirs of James Johnson).
14 Feb. 1854.

Johnson, Jesse
    pp. 111-2. Petition of William W. Johnson, admr.,
for an order to sell land for payment of debts of
the estate. Heirs are sons and daughters of dec'd.:
        William W. Johnson
        Emanuel Johnson
        Rachael A. Johnson
        Lousia A. Johnson, minor
        Elizabeth Johnson, minor
        Julia A. Johnson, minor
        James H. Johnson, minor
        Lydia Johnson, minor
        Frances Johnson, minor
        Laura Johnson, minor
        Jesse Johnson, minor

Infant not named
Sarah Johnson, widow of dec'd.
10 July 1854.
p. 113. Authorized to sell land, subjecr to widow's
dower. 11 Sept. 1854.
pp. 190-1. Appraisal of real and personal property by
commissioners. 14 Aug. 1854.

Johnson,
Johnston, John
pp. 125-7. Petition of James R. Norton and John W.
Johnson, admrs., for sale of land (except the part
allotted as dower of Mary Johnson, widow of John Johnson)
for division to heirs listed below with the exception
of:
James Johnson, Cato Springs, Miss. not included.
Children of Mary Ann Anderson, dec'd. listed as
John, Margaret, Mary, Russell, Samuel and George
G. W. and J. T. Anderson not included in this
document. 31 July 1854
p. 241-3. Petition of James R. Norton and John W.
Johnson to divide slaves to heirs:
Mary Johnson, relict of dec'd.
Margaret, wife of James R. Norton
Sealy (or Celia), wife of Robert E. Price
Molsey Grantham's heirs, to-wit:
John Grantham and Edward Grantham
Prudence Grantham's heirs, to-wit:
Johnson Grantham, Daniel Grantham and Mary
Grantham
Patience, wife of M. M. Watson
John W. Johnson
George W. Johnson
Elizabeth, widow of William Williams, Horry Dist.,
South Carolina
Mary Anderson's, to-wit:
John J. Anderson, Margaret K. Anderson, Morgan
(Maryann?) Anderson, David R. Anderson, S. O.
Anderson, J. T. Anderson, G. W. Anderson and
G. J. Anderson, Horry Dist., South Carolina.
Jane, wife of Joseph Griffin, Horry Dist., S. C.
James Johnson, Cato Springs, Miss.
26 Dec. 1854.
p. 393. Return on the sale of slaves. 26 Mar. 1855.
pp. 682-3. Return of James R. Norton and John W.
Johnston, admrs. 18 Feb. 1856.
pp. 684-5. Partial settlement to heirs listed above
with the the exception of Mrs. Mary Johnston, widow of
the dec'd. is not included. 24 Mar. 1854.

Johnson, Richard M.
p. 543. Bond of Amanda J. Johnson as admr. of the

estate of Richard M. Johnson, dec'd. Bonds: C. J.
M. Andrews and John W. Johnson. 21 Dec. 1855.

Johnson, William L.
pp. 142-3. Inventory and appraisal of personal property
of William L. Johnson, dec'd. J. W. Johnson, admr.
10 July 1854.

Jones, Henry
p. 131. Return of Ellen (Elender) Jones, admr. of
the estate of Henry Jones. 12 June 1854.
p. 180. Inventory of the estate, Elender Jones, admx.
24 July 1854.

Jones, Martha Jernigan
pp. 164-5. Return of James E. Gachet, guardian of
Martha Jernigan Jones. 28 July 1854.
pp. 589-91. Annual return of guardian. 23 Oct. 1855.

Jones, Samuel
pp. 100-1. Return Joseph Jones, excr. of the estate
of Samuel Jones and guardian of:
Thomas Jones
Samuel Jones
Derrill Jones
Benjamin Jones
Henry D. Clayton appointed guardian ad Litem of minors.
3 May 1854.

Jordan. Horatio
p. 490. Resignation of J. S. Williams as admr. of the
estate of Horatio Jordan. 9 Oct. 1855.

Ketcham, David
p. 124. Bond of Bartley W. Ketcham as admr. of the
estate of David Ketcham. dec'd. Bondsmen: Hart McCall,
John M. Westbrook, David H. Ketcham and J. W. Faulk.
Mary Ketcham, widow of the dec'd., notified of this
application. 8 Nov. 1854.
pp. 268-9. Inventory and appraisal of the estate by
commissioners. 25 Nov. 1854.
p. 274. Petition of Bartley W. Ketcham to sell personal
property for the purpose of paying debts of the estate.
29 Nov. 1854.
pp. 523-6. Petition of Bartley W. Ketcham to sell land
for division to heirs:
Mary Ann Ketcham, the widow
Ann Eliza Ketcham
Bartley W. Ketcham
Mary Caroline, wife of J. W. Faulk
Sarah Ann, wife of John M. (or N.?) Westbrook
David H. Ketcham
Elizabeth Jane Ketcham, minor
Gilbert M. D. L. Ketcham. minor

Cloe Matilda, wife of Henry Casey
Benjamin F. Ketcham, minor
13 Dec. 1854.
p. 540. Return of sales of real and personal property,
B. W. Ketcham, admr. 15 Dec. 1855.

Key, Caroline G.
p. 641. Russell County (Ala.) The will of Caroline G.
Key offered for probate by attorney for Americus C.
Mitchell. Ordered that the case be continued in the
October term of court. William E. Barnett appointed
guardian ad Litem of minor heirs. 27 Sept. 1855.
p. 641. Russell Co., Crawford, (Ala.). The probation
of will rejected on the grounds that the decedent was
not of sound mind at the time of her death.
12 Nov. 1855.
p. 642. Letters of administration issued to Americus
C. Mitchell as the husband of Caroline G. Key did not
apply as admr. Bondsmen: Catherine Mitchell and John
L. Daniel.
pp. 643-4. Inventory and appraisal of estate.
26 Nov. 1855.

Kilpatrick, Benjamin R.
p. 441. Bond of James L. Shipman as admr. of the estate
of Benjamin R. Kilparrick. Bondsmen: George R. Scroggins
and John McDonald. 10 Sept. 1855.
p. 471. Inventory and appraisal of personal property
by commissioners. 3 Oct. 1855.

King, Caroline
pp. 98-100. Annual return of William L. Cowen, guardian
of:
    Sheppard W. King
    Marshall King
minor heirs of Caroline King, dec'd. 2 May 1854.

King, Gary
pp. 84-5. Return of Winney Rumley, guardian of:
    Nancy King
    Nicey King
minor heirs of Gary King, dec'd. 14 Mar. 1854.

King, Harvey
pp. 652-3. Will of Harvey King
    Wife: Sarah King
    Children of William King
        Anna King
        Richard King
        Sarah Harvey King
    Excr: Sarah King
    Wit: Reubin Allison, R. L. Butt, W. M. Lewis
        and J. B. Simpson.

Date: 21 Jan. 1856
Recorded: 10 Mar. 1856
p. 654. R. J. Garrington appointed guardian ad Litem of:

William King	Richard King
Anna King	Sarah King

10 Mar. 1856.
p. 655. Letters testamentary issued in favor of Sarah King, widow of Harvey King. 10 Mar. 1856.
pp. 673-6. Inventory and appraisal of estate.
1 Apr. 1856.

King, Henry
p. 27. Petition of Abi King, widow of Henry King, for letters of administration for the estate. Ordered that Abi King be appointed admx. 7 June 1854.
p. 28. Bond of Abi King as admx. of the estate. Bondsmen: George J. Turman and Allen Eiland. 13 June 1854.
p. 40. Petition of Abi King, admx., to sell a portion of perishable property. 26 June 1854.
pp. 94-7. Inventory and appraisal of the estate.
24 July 1854.
pp. 188-90. Account of sale of personal property.
14 Aug. 1854.
p. 199. Bond of Abi King as guardian of Nancy Miriam King, under the age 14, minor heir of Henry King. Bondsmen: Allen Eiland and Absolom Eiland. 8 Dec. 1854.
p. 200. ibid, Lewis Hilliard King
p. 204. Bond Abi King as admx. Bondsmen: Harvey King and George J. Turman. 13 Dec. 1854.
p. 227. Macon Co., Ala. Deed of gift of slaves from Henry King at his death to his son Lewis Hilliard King. Abner H. King is to be guardian of said Lewis Hilliard King. 8 Jan. 1851. (Recorded in CONVEYANCE RECORD BOOK "H", p. 13, Apr. 1851).
p. 228. Macon Co., Ala. Abi King presents to court a paper purporting to be a deed and makes suit to have same admitted to probate as the Last Will of Henry King, who died 28 Dec. 1850. The following given citation to appear at court to contest said application:
Abner H. King
Tandy W. King
Ann E. Cadenhead, gr-dau. in right of Sarah S.
Nancy M. King
Lewis H. King
26 June 1854.
p. 229. Case continued until the next term of court.
14 Sept. 1854.
p. 229. Ordered that the said instrument be admitted to probate as Last Will and Testament of Henry.
Further ordered that letters of admr. be issued to Abi King. 19 Oct. 1854.
p. 263. Petition of Abi King for division of personal property. Heirs are:

Abner H. King
Robert H. King
Tandy W. King
Sarah Elizabeth Cadenhead
Nancy Miriam King
Lewis Hilliard King
1 Nov. 1854.
pp. 275-7. Commissioners report personal property of
the estate cannot be equally divided. 6 Nov. 1854.
p. 355. Abner H. King, guardian of Ann Elizabeth Cadenhead, states he has received s sum of money from Homer
S. Crowder, admr. of the estate of James Cadenhead, of
Macon County, Ala., and it is the only property effects
that has come into his hands for the said ward.
18 Jan. 1855.
pp. 518-21. Petition of Abi King, guardian of Nancy
Miriam and Lewis Hilliard King, to sell land belonging
to the minors for the purpose of investing the proceeds.
11 Dec. 1855.

Lamar, H. (Harmong)
p. 225. Annual return of R. H. Howard and James E.
Barnett, excrs . of the estate of Harmong Lamar *.
pp. 226-7. Heirs:
John O. Lamar
Cornelia, wife of Robert Howard
Lucy, wife of James E. Barnett
William H. Lamar
Lucius Lamar
Martha A. Lamar, minor
Thomas Lamar, minor
Sarah E. Lamar, minor
7 Aug. 1854.

Lamb, Jacob
pp. 70-3. Return of J. M. Lampley, admr. List of
heirs:
Charlott, wife of Littleton Morgan, Ball Hill, Ga.
Ann Eliza, wife of James Ayers, Ball Hill, Ga.
Mary, wife of L. L. Peacock, Ball Hill, Ga.
Temperance (Malinda?), wife of Uriah Moss
Hamburg, Perry Co., Ala.
Basheba, wife of John B. Beck, Brownville, Ark.
Elizabeth, wife of J. F. Lacy, Villuda, Ala.
W. A. B. Lamb, Sparta, Ala.
A. J. Lamb, Sparta, Ala.
Madison Lamb, Sparta, Ala.
28 Apr. 1854.
p. 395. Return of sale of land. 10 Feb. 1855.
pp. 396-7. List of heirs in final settlement as above
with the following exceptions:

* ABSTRACTS OF WILLS & ESTATES BOOK II, Will of H. Lamar.

Basheba, wife of John B. Beck not listed
Analizer, wife of James B. Ayers, Villuda, Ala.
J. G. Lamb, Hamburg, Ala.
Jackson Lamb, Sparta, Ala.
Mary, wife of L. L. Peacock, Ft. Browder, Ala.
10 Feb. 1855.

Langford, Robert
p. 216. Return of Edward C. Bullock, admr.
pp. 217-8. Final settlement to heirs:
Sarah Langford, widow of dec'd., now Sarah Harwell
Frances, wife of David A. Thompson, a dau.
S. J., wife of B. S. Covington, a dau.
Mary, wife of Jackson Averett, a dau.
Robert Langford, Talbot Co., Ga., a son
Edward Langford, Talbot Co., Ga., a son
10 July 1854.

Laws, George, Sr. *
Will of George Laws, Sr. Planter
Claramount County, South Dist., S. C.
Children: William Laws   Jared Laws
James Laws   Robert Laws
Isaiah Laws   John Laws
George Laws   David Laws
Henry Laws   Nancy Brown
Excrs: Sons, James, Isaiah, George and Henry Laws
Wit: James R. Laws, James Watson, William Barkley
and Samuel J. Taylor
Date: 17 June 1826.
Recorded: 2 Mar. 1829 in Sumter Dist., S. C.
19 June 1841 in Marin (Marion?) Co., Ga.
Book "A", Folio 5.
13 Feb. 1853 in Barbour Co., Ala.

Lee, Needham, Sr.
p. 166. Petition of D. M. McKinzie and Lovard Lee, Jr.,
to sell personal property, except the slaves for
division to heirs. 25 Sept. 1854
p. 195. Bond of William King as guardian of:
Martha Ann Lee
over the age of 14. Bondsmen: Daniel McKenzie and
Levi Faulk. 28 Nov. 1854.
p. 196. ibid, Mary Jane Lee
p. 196. ibid, Christopher Columbus Lee
p. 197. Bond of Sarah Ann Lee as guardian of:
Sarah A. Lee
28 Nov. 1854.
p. 197. ibid, Winford Lee
pp. 239-40. Petition of Daniel McKenzie and Lovard Lee,
excrs., to divide property as was provided in the will

* Recorded in: CONVEYANCE RECORD BOOK "K", p. 587.

of Needham, Sr. Heirs are:
    Sally Lee, widow of dec'd.
    Martha Lee, a dau.
    Sally Lee, a dau.
    Wineford Lee, a dau.
Commissioners appointed to divide slaves and land.
17 Oct. 1854.
pp. 291-2. Commissioners report on division of slaves
to heirs. 13 Nov. 1854.
pp. 305-7. Petition of Daniel McKenzie and Lovard
Lee, Jr., to sell land for equal division to heirs.
18 Nov. 1854.
pp. 610-15. Final return of excrs. of the estate.
3 Jan. 1856.
pp. 616-8. Distribution of estate to heirs:
    John W. Jacksin, in right of his wife Elizabeth
    Needham Lee, Jr.
    G. H. Hudson, in right of his wife Louisiana
    Lovard Lee, Jr.
    Martha A., wife of James W. Stokes, Abbeville, Ala.
    Columbus Lee, minor
    Jane Lee, minor
    Sarah Lee, minor
    Wineford Lee, minor
    Heirs of John Lee, Jefferson Co., Ga., names
                not known
    Sarah Lee, the widow
18 Feb. 1856.
pp. 691-3. Return of William King, guardian of:
    Columbus Lee and Jane Lee
11 Feb. 1856.

Lewis, Zachariah M. D. L.
    pp. 438-9. Bond of Hanson and Jane Lewis as admrs. of
    the estate of Zachariah M. D. L. Lewis, dec'd. Bonds-
    man: William Lewis. 30 Aug. 1855
    p. 476. Inventory and Appraisal of real and personal
    property by commissioners. 15 Oct. 1855.
    pp. 640-1. Return of sale of cotton. 23 Feb. 1856.

Locke, Richard
    p. 185. Annual return of Jesse Locke, guardian of
    M. B. Locke. 8 June 1854. (Heir of Richard Locke).

Lovitt, Joshua
    p. 487. Bond of Henry T. Wilkinson as admr. of the
    estate of Joshua Lovitt. Bondsmen: Hugh Cameron and
    W. W. Wilkinson. 8 Oct. 1855.
    pp. 584-6. Final return of Thomas S. Locke, admr.,
    with Henry T. Wilkinson, the present admr.
    8 Oct. 1855.

Lowman, Joseph
    p. 167. Petition of Mary H. Lowman to divide slaves

to heirs:
     Martha Elizabeth, wife of James L. Lowman
     John David Lowman
     William George Lowman
     Mary Susan Lowman
     Sarah Ann Catherine Lowman
     Benjamin Joseph Lowman
     Samuel Anderson Lowman
     Eugene Henry Lowman
All minors except Martha Elizabeth Lowman.
p. 168. Authorized to divide slaves. 27 Sept. 1854.
p. 297. Report of commissioners that slaves of the
estate cannot be equally divided without a sale.
20 Nov. 1854.
p. 414. Bond of Seaborn Jones as admr. de bonis non
of the estate. Bondsmen: Isham C. Browder and Wilson
M. Bates. 31 May 1855.
p. 485. ibid, 18 Oct. 1855,
p. 645. Bond of James L. Shipman as guardian of:
     Henry E. Lowman
under the age of 14 years. Bondsmen: W. H. Boswell
and John J. Lowman. 28 Feb. 1856.
pp. 645-6. ibid, Samuel A. Lowman
p. 646. Bond of Seaborn Jones as guardian of:
     Sarah Ann Lowman
Bondsmen: James L. Lowman and John L. Lowman.
28 Feb. 1856.
p. 647. ibid, Mary S. Lowman.

Mann, Gilbert
     p. 103. Bond of Daniel M. Seals as admr. of the
     estate of Gilbert Mann, dec'd. Bondsman: H. D. Clayton.
     Robert Mann, son of the dec'd., is the only next of kin
     and he consents to the above admr. 27 July 1854.
     p. 109. Return of Daniel M. Seals, guardian of Gilbert
     Mann, non compos mentis, who died intestate. Robert
     Mann is sole heir. The admr. petitions for a final
     settlement. 27 July 1854.
     p. 116. Apraisal and inventory of personal property
     by commissioners. 5 Oct. 1854.
     pp. 121-2 Petition of Robert Mann, son of Gilbert
     Mann, a person of about 80 years old and due to his
     advanced age he is in an imbecile state of mind. Robert
     Mann ask the court to determine the sanity of Gilbert
     Mann. The verdict of the court was that he is non
     compos mentis. 10 May 1854.
     p. 311. Petition of D. M. Seals, admr., to sell a
     portion of land to pay debts of the estate. 20 Nov. 1854.

Martin, minors
     p. 544. Delila George Martin and Delphia Thomas Martin
     nominate Michael Chesnut as their gurardian.
     p. 544. Bond of Michael Chesnut as guardian of:
     Delila G. Martin

minor over the age of 14 years. Bondsmen: Horatio J. Marley, William King and John P. McNair. 21 Dec. 1855. p. 545. ibid, Delphia T. Martin.

Martin, Gibson

    p. 379. Bond of Seth Mabrey as guardian of Mary J. Martin, minor heir of Gibson Martin. Bondsman: R. H. Fryer. 10 Mar. 1855.
    p. 380. ibid, Sarah E. Martin
    p. 380. ibid, Henry F. Martin
    p. 381. ibid, Seleta O. Martin
    p. 382. ibid, Martha V. Martin
    10 Mar. 1855.

Martin, James L.

    pp. 42-3. Final return of R. E. Price, guardian of:
        George W. Martin
    heir of James L. Martin, who has now attained his majority. 7 Feb. 1854.
    pp. 47-8. Return of Harrell F. Reaves, guardian of:
        Sarah Jane Martin
        Harriet Martin
    31 Jan. 1854.
    p. 48. Annual return of James Orr, guardian of:
        Mary A. Martin
        Victoria C. Martin
    31 Jan. 1854.
    pp. 156-7. Petition of Seth Mabery, admr., to make deed titles to:
        Sarah Martin   Francis M. Martin
        John F. Martin   William H. Martin
    for land bought by them from the estate.
    24 Aug. 1854.
    p. 632. Return of Harrel F. Reaves, guardian.
    19 Jan. 1856.
    p. 666. Annual return of James Orr, guardian.
    15 Feb. 1856.

Martin, John H.

    pp. 7-8. Return of Thomas J. Lasiter, admr., and files accounts and vouchers for final settlement with the creditors of the estate of John H. Martin, the estate heretofore declared insolvent. The deo'd. left a widow, two sons and a daughter, not named. The children are minors. 9 Feb. 1854.

Maxwell, Green L., minor

    p. 170. Bond of James W. Norton as guardian of Green L. Maxwell, minor. Bondsmen: Andrew G. Neely and George W. Barker. 13 Oct. 1854.
    pp. 303-4. Inventory of property by James W. Norton. 1 Jan. 1855.
    p. 665. Return of guardian, James W. Norton. 29 Mar. 1856.

McBride, John (Sr.)
>pp. 67-70. Return of James P. McBride, excr. List
>of heirs:
>>Samuel McBride
>>James P. McBride
>>Mary, wife of Samuel Vining
>>Sarah, widow of Jeremiah Walton
>>Catherine, widow of Jacob Nelson
>>Elizabeth, wife of Dr. N. N. Smith, living in Ga.
>>Heirs of Jane Vining, dec'd.:
>>>Rachael Glover, wife of Thomas Glover
>>>David J. Vining, of full age, living in Ga.
>>>Washington Vining, of full age, living in Ga.
>>>Jackson L. Vining, minor
>>>Eliza J. Vining, minor
>>>William M. Vining, minor
>>>George B. Vining, minor
>>>Sarah A. Vining, minor
>>>Ann Vining, minor
>30 Jan. 1854.
>pp. 386-7. Return of James P. and Samuel McBride,
>excrs. 12 Feb. 1855.
>pp. 388-9. Heirs listed in final settlement given
>above. Elizabeth Smith is listed as Eliz.,wife of
>Dr. Smith, LaGrange, Ga. 26 Mar. 1855.
>pp. 703-4. Return of James P. McBride, guardian of:
>>Eliza Vining   Sarah Vining
>>William Vining   Anne Vining
>>George Vining
>11 Feb. 1856.

McBride, John (Jr.)
>pp. 2-4. Annual return of Mary A. Vining, guardian of:
>>John McBride   Mary Agnes McBride
>>Eliza McBride   Sophia J. McBride
>13 Feb. 1854.
>pp. 20-1. Final settlement of Mary A. Vining with
>Sarah C. McBride, now the wife of E. P. Woods.
>13 Mar. 1854.
>p. 27. Bond of James P. McBride as guardian of:
>>Mary A. McBride   Elizabeth McBride
>>Sophia J. McBride
>Bondsmen: James Bigham, Samuel McBride and Catherine
>J. Nelson. 6 June 1854.
>p. 35. Petition of Mary A. Vining for a guardian of
>her children:
>>Sophia J. McBride   Eliza McBride
>>Mary A. McBride
>14 Apr. 1854.
>p. 338. Return of James P. McBride, guardian.
>14 Aug. 1854.
>p. 390. Return of James P. McBride, guardian.
>12 Feb. 1855.
>p. 630, ibid, 11 Feb. 1856.

McCall, Joanna
> p. 175. Bond of Duncan McCall as guardian of:
>   Roderick H. H. McCall
minor heir of Joanna McCall, dec'd. Bondsmen: John
W. Clark and John C. McNab. 17 Nov. 1854.
> p. 444. Bond as guardian of Duncan McCall for Roderick
H. H. McCall. Bondsmen: Daniel A. McCall and Ransom
Godwin. 19 Sept. 1855.
> p. 545. Resignation of Duncan McCall as guardian of
his son, Roderick H. H. McCall. He requests the appoint-
ment of Gilbert McCall as guardian. 21 Dec. 1855.
> pp. 561-2. Bond of Gilbert McCall as guardian of:
Roderick H. H. McCall. Bondsmen: D. A. McCall and
Roderick McCall. 7 Jan. 1856.
> p. 650. Inventory and appraisal of the property of
Roderick H. H. McCall, minor. 29 Feb. 1856.

McCracken, Robert
> p. 168. Will of Robert McCracken
>   Wife: Mary McCracken
>   Sons: James W. McCracken
>   William McCracken
>   John M. McCracken
>   Daus: Ann, wife of Thomas J. Ellis
>   Catherine McCracken
>   Mentions money from the estate of James McCracken,
>   in South Carolina
>   Excrs: Green Stephen and James Gary
>   Wit: A. P. Parrott, John F. Comer and
>   John Jimmerson.
>   Date: 14 May 1854
>   Recorded: 11 Sept. 1854.
> p. 169. All children are of full age except William,
John M., and Catherine. Henry D. Clayton appointed
guardian ad Litem of minors. 10 July 1854
> p. 340. Resignation of Green Stephen and James Gary
as excrs. of the estate. 28 Oct. 1854.
> p. 369. Petition of Thomas S. Locke, admr., to sell
personal property except that which was specifically
willed to the family. 3 Mar. 1855.
> p. 370. Mary McCracken, widow of the dec'd., files
her dissent to her husband's Last Will and Testament
and claims such portion of the estate as she would
have been entitled in the event he had died intestate.
5 Mar. 1855.
> p. 423. Petition of Mary McCracken for her dower.
Heirs are:
>   Ann, wife of Thomas J. Ellis, Stewart Co., Ga.
>   William D. McCracken, minor
>   John M. McCracken, minor
>   Mary Catherine McCracken, minor
5 Mar. 1855
> p. 424. Commissioners summoned to set off dower, which

is land and dwelling house in Barbour County.
14 May 1855.
p. 425. Report of commissioners that dower claims
were set off. 8 June 1855.
p. 425. Dower allotted to petitioner. 11 June 1855.
pp. 538-9. Return of sale of personal property, Seth
Mabrey, admr. 26 Nov. 1855.
pp. 578-9. Petition of John W. Clark, admr., to sell
real estate, less the widow's dower, as the personal
property is insufficient to pay debts of the estate.
14 Jan. 1856.
pp. 592-3. Final settlement of Thomas S. Locke, admr.,
with John W. Clark, present admr. 8 Oct. 1855.

McCrary, James
pp. 242-3. Return of William King, admr. List of
heirs given below. 10 July 1854.
pp. 244-5. Final settlement to heirs:
Rebecca McCrary, the widow
Thomas McCrary, a son
Alexander McCrary, a son
Sarah, wife of A. F. McKinney, a dau.
Francis (Frances) McCrary, a dau.
Warren McCrary, minor son
James J. McCrary, minor son
Letha McCrary minor dau.
14 Nov. 1854.
pp. 346-7. Petition of William King, admr., to sell
real estate for distribution among heirs, except a
a portion of land reserved as the widow's dower. Heirs
listed as above with these changes:
Alexander McCrary, non resident
Francis (Frances), wife of Frederick Davis,
non resident
Alitha McCrary, minor
Ann McCrary, minor
James McCrary (Sr.) died in the possession of a land
warrant issued to him by the U. S. Government.
p. 348. Commissioners appointed to investigate the
necessity of sale of land for equal division.
25. Nov. 1854.
p. 349. Ordered by the court that the admr. sell
land and the land warrant. 25 Nov. 1854.

McDonald, Alexander
p. 134. Return of John Gill Shorter, admr. de Bonis
non of the estate of Alexander McDonald. Heirs are:
Mary M. O. Harper
Sarah Jane H. Harper
Martha G. G. Harper
Robert McDonald W. Harper
Ferinand A. L. Harper
James L. W. Harper

minors. Henry D. Clayton appointed guardian ad Litem
of minors. 22 July 1854.
pp. 465-6. Return of John Gill Shorter, admr.
25 June 1855.

McDonald, Daniel B.
     p. 442. Bond of John McDonald as admr. of the estate
of Daniel B. McDonald, dec'd. Bondsmen: Daniel McKenzie
and John McKenzie. 15 Sept. 1855.
     p. 498. Inventory and appraisal of property by the
commissioners. 5 Nov. 1855.
     p. 700. Return of John McDonald, admr., on the sale
of cotton. 21 Apr. 1856.

     Neel,
     Neal,
McDonald, Neil,
     p. 316. Petition of Daniel McKenzie, admr., for
division of slaves to heirs:
          Mary McDonald, widow of dec'd.
          Sarah McDonald, minor
          Mary McDonald, minor
          Eufenia McDonald, minor
          Celia Ann McDonald, minor
          Neally McDonald, minor
Commissioners appointed to divide slaves.
29 Nov. 1854.
     p. 316. Report of commissioners that slaves cannot be
equally divided without a sale. 11 Dec. 1854.
     pp. 317-8. Petition of Mary McDonald for her dower
which is land in Barbour County. 20 Dec. 1854.
     p. 319. Return report of comminnioners that dower
claims were set off. Ordered by court that the report
of commissioners be recorded and petitioner allotted
dower claims. 20 Dec. 1854.
     pp. 353-4. Petition of Daniel McKenzie, admr., for
sale of land for division among heirs, alleging that
the widow is entitled to her dower. Heirs listed above
with the exception Eufenia McDonald is not included
in this document. 29 Nov. 1854.
     p. 355. The admr. authorized to sell land.
11 Dec. 1854.

McGilvary, Janet
     p. 655. Will of Janet McGilvary
          Nephew: Roderick C. Chisholm "whole estate".
                    Said Roderick C. Chisholm shall give to
                    his sister, Janett, $50.
          Excr: Roderick C. Chisholm
          Wit: Peter Stewart and Thomas Harris
          Date: 2 Dec. 1848.
          Recorded: 10 Mar. 1856.

McKay, Donald
     p. 194. Bond of Winney McKay and Alexander McRae as

admrs. of the estate of Donald McKay, dec'd. Bondsmen: F. A. McRae and Jacob Utsey. 28 Nov. 1854.
pp. 299-300. Inventory and appraisal of estate by
commissioners. 28 Dec. 1854.

McLane,
McLean, Daniel

p. 304. Bond of Duncan McGilvary as admr. of the
estate of Daniel McLean. Bondsmen: Hart McCall,
Clark Echols, William W. Johnson, John McGilvary
and John C. McNab. 1 Jan. 1855.
p, 313. Petition of Duncan McGilvary, admr., to sell
perishable property. 5 Jan. 1855.
pp. 515-8. Petition of Duncan McGilvary, admr., to
sell land for equal division to the brothers and
sisters of the dec'd., to-wit:

    John McLane
    Hugh McLane
    Libby McLane
    Christian Cameron, a married woman residing in
                the Province of Canada.

17 Oct. 1855.
p. 539. Petition of Duncan McGilvary, admr., to sell
slaves for equal distribution among heirs:
p. 540. John McLean
      Hugh McLean
      Libby McLean
      Christian, wife of John Cameron, living in
      upper Canada, postoffice is Alexandria
26 Nov. 1855.
pp. 574-5. Return of Duncan McGilvary on the sales
of real and personal property. 14 Jan. 1856.

McLeod, Daniel D.

p. 628. Petition of John K. Norton to sell perishable
property of the estate. 11 Feb. 1856.

McLeod, Lindsey

pp. 282-4. Will of Lindsey McLeod
    Wife: Smitha McLeod
    Son: Daniel McLeod
    Excr: William Hinson
    Wit: Daniel B. Bridges, Lemuel Hinson and
           William H. C. Gibson.
    Date: 4 Aug. 1854.
    Recorded: 13 Nov. 1854.

McMillan,
McMillian, Alexander

p. 573. Bond of Edward C. Bullock as admr. of the
estate of Alexander McMillian. Bondsmen: J. L. Pugh
and A. McKenzie. 21 Nov. 1855.

McMillan
McMillian, Daniel
>p. 201. Bond of Fairly (Finlay?) McMillan as guardian
>of John McMillian, minor heir of Daniel McMillian.
>Bondsmen: Mary McMillan, Archibald Carmichael and
>A. H. King. 11 Dec. 1854.
>p. 202. ibid, Edward McMillan
>p. 203. ibid, Charles McMillian
>pp. 281-2. Return of Mary and Finlay McMillan, guardians
>of Fairly, John, Edward and Charles McMillan.
>13 Nov. 1854.
>pp. 350-2. Accounts filed for final settlement to heirs:
>>Mary McMillan, widow of dec'd.
>>Finlay McMillan, a son
>>Fairly McMillan, a son
>>Charles McMillan, a son
>>John McMillan, a son
>>Edward McMillan, a son
>13 Nov. 1854.

McNab, Duncan
>p. 438. Bond of John McNab as admr. of the estate
>of Duncan McNab. Bondsman: John Gill Shorter.
>22 Aug. 1855.
>pp. 509-14. Inventory and appraisal of estate, John
>McNab, admr. 22 Nov. 1855.

McPhail, Edward C.
>p. 648. Bond of Effy Williams as admx. of the estate
>of Edward C. McPhail, dec'd. Bondsmen: E. C. Holleman
>and Z. J. Daniel. 29 Feb. 1856.

Mitchell, Benjamin J. J.
>p. 532. Bond of Sarah G. Mitchell as admx. of the
>estate of Benjamin J. J. Mitchell. Bondsman: Randolph
>Mitchell. 7 Dec. 1855.

Moore, John C., minor
>pp. 24-5. Final settlement of John Gill Shorter,
>guardian, in account with John C. Moore, minor, who
>has now attained his majority. 19 May. 1854.

Moore, John W.
>pp. 135-6. Return of Jesse Locke, guardian of James
>P. Moore. 7 June 1854.
>p. 137. ibid, Americus Moore
>pp. 183-5. Final settlement of Jesse Locke, admr. of
>the estate of John W. Moore, dec'd. Heirs:
>>William B. Moore, minor son
>>Americus Moore, minor son
>>James P. Moore, minor son
>>Mary E. Moore, minor dau.
>8 June 1854.

p. 446. Annual settlement of A. T. Dawkins, guardian
of: William B. Moore
        Mary Ella Moore
30 June 1855.
pp. 565-7. Petition of Jesse Locke, guardian of James
P. Moore, to sell a slave for reinvestment.
26 Nov. 1855.
p. 568. Authorized to sell slave. 3 Jan. 1856.

Nash, Acton
pp. 408-9. Will of Acton Nash
Wife: Margaretta Nash
Son: Reubin A. Nash
Dau: Elizabeth Hardy
Gr-dau: Susanna B. Hardy
Excr: Reubin A. Nash
Wit: Hiram Kinchen, James W. Watkins and A. E. Nash
Date: 6 Nov. 1851.
Recorded: 19 Aug. 1854.
pp. 409-12. Clark Echols, James B. R. Smith and Hilliard
Glover, heirs at law, object to the admission to record
the will of Acton Nash, stating that the testator was
not in a proper state of mind and undue influence was
excerised. It was also said that the will was not read
to the testator before he signed it. 12 Feb. 1855.
p. 411. On 21 Feb. 1855 A. E. Nash gave his deposition
in Twiggs County, Georgia.
p. 412. Will of Acton Nash was read to him in the
presence of:
Reubin Nash
Margaret (Margaretta?) Nash
Mrs. E. Hardy
Susan B. Hardy, now Mrs. Hawkins
Mr. Nash was between eighty and ninety years old at
the time the will was read. 20 Mar. 1855.
p. 412. Legal notice given to the following to appear
at court:
James B. R. Smith and wife, Barbara
Clark Echols and wife, Hester
H. Y. Glover and wife, Sarah
Margarett Nash, widow of dec'd.
Reubin A. Nash
Jacob B. Nash
Thomas Nash
William Rainy and wife, Fedina
20 Mar. 1855.

Nelson, J. B.
pp. 10-12. Final return of Eli S. Shorter, admr., the
estate heretofore declared insolvent, and files
accounts and vouchers for distribution among creditors.
6 Mar. 1854.

Newman, James, minor
> p. 123. Bond of Michael Currin as guardian of James
> Newman, minor. Bondsman: Robert T. White.
> 6 Nov. 1854.
> p. 215. Resignation of Michael Currin as guardian.
> 6 Nov. 1854.

Norton, William V.
> p. 37. Return of James R. Norton, guardian of:
>> Delila A. Norton   Urban (Erban) W. Norton
>> Nancy A. Norton   Franklin W. Norton
>> Tolbot (Tolbert) M. Norton   Thomas C. Norton
>
> 11 Feb. 1854.
> p. 392. Final return of James R. Norton, guardian
> of Nancy Ann Norton, now the wife of N. A. Petty.
> 12 Feb. 1855.

O'Brien,
O'Bryan, Jeremiah
> p. 104. Bond of Martin H. Joyce as admr. of the estate
> of Jeremiah O'Bryan, dec'd. Bondsmen: Emanuel Poston
> and Thomas Robinson. 24 Aug. 1854.
> pp 270-3. Inventory and appraisal of personal
> property of J. O'Brien by commissioners. 8 Dec. 1854.
> pp. 453-8. Statement of goods and chattel of the
> estate of Jere O'Brien, Martin H. Joyce, admr.
> 5 July 1855.
> p. 459. Petition of Martin H. Joyce, admr., to declare
> the estate insolvent. 13 Aug. 1855.
> p. 460. Estate declared insolvent and the admr.
> authorized to make settlement of accounts. 13 Aug. 1855.

Odom, Theophilus
> Will of Theophilus Odom * , Marlborough Dist., S. C.
>> Wife: Catharine Odom
>> Sons: Peter Odom
>>> Robert Odom
>>> Thomas Odom
>>
>> Daus: Mary Newton
>>> Margaret Newton
>>> Lucy Ann McNab
>>> Elizabeth Kennedy
>>> Amelia Odom
>>> Catharine Odom
>>> Francis (Frances Odom)
>>> Isabella Odom
>>
>> Friend: Anderson Newton
>> Excrs: Peter Odom and Anderson Newton, of
>>> Marborough Dist.
>>
>> Wit: S. J. Townsend, J. G. Dudley and
>>> W. D. Wallace.

* Recorded in CONVEYANCE RECORD BOOK "Q". pp. 695-7.

Date: 12 Dec. 1855.
Recorded: 24 Dec. 1856, Marborough Dist., S. C.
14 Dec. 1863, Barbour County, Ala.

Oliver, Milbra
p. 46. Report of commissioners on division of
slaves, McDonald Oliver, admr. 9 Jan. 1854.

Oliver, Wiley
pp 21-3. Report of division of slaves. 9 Jan. 1854.
pp. 397-9. Final return of McDonald Oliver, admr.
p. 400. Heirs:
Milbry Oliver, dec'd., late widow. The admr. is
to pay her share to the admr. of her estate.
William Oliver, a son
McDonald Oliver
Sarah, wife of John L. Roberts
Jasper N. Oliver, minor
Henry Y. Oliver, minor
A. R. (Alexander) Oliver, minor
14 Feb. 1855.

Patterson, Celia
Will of Celia Paterson *
County of Rockingham, State of North Carolina
Sons: Turner D. Patterson
William C. Patterson
Children of Turner D. Paterson (not named)
Gr-daus: Julia a Patterson
Manerva Celia Patterson
Mary E. Dick
Gr-sons: Joseph B. Holerly
Victor M. Holderly
Mentions Bartlett Patterson and Delany L. D.
Patterson.
Excr: Friend, Daniel E. Guerrant
Wit: Booker J. Lelland and G. H. Holderly
Date: 19 June 1854
Recorded: 4 Aug. 1856 in Barbour County, (Ala.)

Peake, Virginia
p. 209. Return of J. D. Johns(t)on, guardian of
Virginia Peak. 10 July 1854.

Pendergrass, Simeon
p. 486. Bond of Daniel M. Seals as admr. of the estate
of Simeon Pendergrass, dec'd. Bondsman: Joseph A.
Holland. 8 Oct. 1855.

Perry, Burrell G.
p. 198. Bond of Sanders C. Echols as guardian of
Mary C. Perry, over the age of 14 years, minor heir

* Recorded in CONVEYANCE RECORD BOOK "M", p. 636.

of Burrell G. Perry. Bondsmen: Mariana S. Minter
and George W. Cariker. 2 Dec. 1854.

Phillips, H. H.
p. 23. Return of Caroline S. Phillips, guardian of
N. E. K. Phillips, minor heir of H. H. Phillips.
9 Jan. 1854.
p. 378. Annual return of C. S. Phillips, guardian.
Henry D. Clayton appointed guardian ad Litem of
N. E. K. Phillips. 22 Jan. 1855.

Powell, David
p. 102. Bond of Nathan Minshew as admr. of the estate
of David Powell. Bondsmen: Jeremiah Shanks and William
A. Bizzell. 10 July 1854.
p. 142. Petition of Nathan Minshew, admr., to sell
perishable property to pay debts of the estate.
22 July 1854.
p. 143. Inventory and appraisal of personal property
by commissioners. 22 July 1854.
pp. 160-1. Return of the sale of personal property.
11 Sept. 1854.
p. 231. Petition of Nathan Minshew, admr., to sell
land to pay debts of the estate, subject to the widow's
dower. 2 Sept. 1854.
pp. 232-3. Heirs:
    Joseph Powell
    Mary Powell, minor
    Margaret Powell, minor
    Sarah Powell, minor
    Ann Powell, minor
    Matilda Powell, minor
    Epsy Powell, minor
    Caroline Powell, minor
    Becky Ann Powell, minor
    Edy Powell, widow of dec'd.
    Ransom Powell, residing in Dale County
    Catherine, wife of Sylvester Nance
2 Sept. 1854.
p. 234. Authorized to sell land, subject to widow's
dower. 23 Oct. 1854.
p. 300. Return of sale of real estate, Nathan Minshew,
admr. 28 Dec. 1854.
p. 333. Petition of Edy Powell, widow of David Powell,
for dower which consist of land in Barbour County.
11 Sept. 1854.
p. 334. Commissioners appointed to set off dower
claims. 10 Oct. 1854.
p. 335. Return report of commissioners that dower
claims were set off. 11 Dec. 1854.
p. 336 Ordered that certificate and report of commissioners be recorded and dower awarded to petitioner.
11 Dec. 1854.

pp. 553-4. Petition of Nathan Minshew, admr., that the
estate is insolvent. Report follows. 2 Nov. 1855.
p. 555. The estate declared insolvent. 10 Dec. 1855.

Pruett, Henry
>   p. 362. Bond of John T. Pruett as guardian of:
>   Josephine Pruett
> minor heir of Henry Pruett, dec'd. Bondsmen: John
> H. Mealing and Thomas A. Hightower. 3 Jan. 1855.
>   p. 636. Return of J. T. Pruett, guardian.
>   22 Jan. 1856.

Pynes, Fair
>   p. 174. Bond of Francis M. Pynes and Jasper Pynes as
> admrs. of the estate of Fair Pynes. dec'd. Bondsmen:
> W. H. Kilpatrick, John L. Stewart and R. T. White.
> 10 Nov. 1854.
>   pp. 267-8. Petition of F. M. Pynes and Jasper Pynes,
> admrs., to sell personal property for payment of
> debts of the estate. 25 Nov. 1854.
>   p. 268. Heirs:
>   Mary Ann Pynes, widow of dec'd.
>   Luprina, wife of Jesse Clemons *
>   Francis M. Pynes
>   Jasper Pynes
>   Daniel Pynes, minor
>   Lydia Pynes, minor
>   Calista Pynes, minor
>   Ruth Pynes, minor
>   Columbus Pynes, minor
>   Mary Ann Pynes, minor
>   Thadeus Pynes, minor
>   Melissa Pynes, minor
>   25 Nov. 1854.
>   pp. 287-90. List of property appraised by commissioners.
>   15 Dec. 1854.

Rawls, Kelly
>   pp. 40-2. Return of B. F. Foster, guardian of:
>   Sally Ann and Kelly Rawls.
>   13 Feb. 1854.

Reid, John
>   pp. 4-5. Petition of James G. Tison, admr., to sell
> Bounty Land Warrant No. 17486 for division to heirs:
>   James H. Reid
>   Margaret Ann, wife of William Sapp
>   Sophie T. Reid, minor
>   Thomas D. Reid, minor
>   Terza C. Reid, minor

*   FIRST MARRIAGE RECORDS, Barbour Co., Ala.: Lupyna Pynes and
                                                Jesse Clements.

Josiah W. Reid, minor
Caroline T. Reid, minor *
Wyatt Reid, minor
p. 6. Authorized to sell land warrant. 20 Feb. 1854.
pp. 58-9. Annual return of James G. Tison, admr.
21 Feb. 1854.
p. 427. Heirs named as above with the exception of:
    Caroline T. Reid, minor
    Wyatt Reid, minor
are listed in this document. Henry D. Clayton appointed
guardian of minors. 16 Apr. 1855.

Richards, William
    pp. 417-9. Inventory and appraisal of personal property
    by commissioners. List of personal property set apart
    for Matilda Richards, widow of dec'd. 8 June 1855.
    p. 499. Petition of R. H. Dawkins and Monroe Stanford,
    admrs., to sell perishable property of the estate.
    5 Nov. 1855.
    p. 598. Petition of R. H. Dawkins and Monroe Stanford,
    admrs., to distribute slaves among heirs, to-wit:
        Matilda, wife of the dec'd.
        Elenor, wife of Monroe Stanford
        Malinda, wife of Lewis H. Holmes
        Mary M., wife of Robert H. Dawkins
        James M. Richards
        Martha A. Richards
        Thomas J. Richards
        Robert J. Richards
        Elizabeth C. Richards
    19 Nov. 1855.
    p. 599. Commissioners appointed to divide slaves.
    627. Return of sale of land in Henry County by Robert
    H. Dawkins and Monroe Stanford, admrs. 11 Feb. 1856.
    p. 628. Return of sale of slaves. 11 July 1856.
    p. 631. Report of commissioners on the division of
    slaves. 26 Nov. 1855.
    p. 652. Return of sale of cotton. 8 Mar. 1856.

Roberts, William N.
    p. 178. Bond of Henry D. Clayton as guardian of:
        Francis P. Roberts
    minor of William N. Roberts. Bondsman: D. M. Seals.
    24 Nov. 1854.
    p. 250. Resignation and final return of John L
    Roberts, former guardian of Francis P. Roberts.
    D. M. Seals appointed guardian ad Litem. 9 Oct. 1854.

Rouse, Henry
    p. 55. Return of H. D. Clayton, guardian of:
        Mary Rouse and Ann Rouse
    14 Feb. 1854.

*   Not included in this document.

p. 171. Bond of Whitfield Clark as guardian of Ann
Rouse. Bondsman: D. M. Seals. 14 Aug. 1854.
p. 207. Final return of Henry D. Clayton, guardian
of Mary Rouse, who is now the wife of L. H. Brown.
18 June 1854.
p. 208. Final settlement of Henry D. Clayton, who
resigned as guardian of Ann Rouse. 19 June 1854.

Sauls, John
pp. 631-2. Bond of Elijah Padget as guardian of:
John Sauls
minor heir of John Sauls, dec'd. Bondsmen: John D.
Ligget, John W. Smith and William W. Stephens.
25 Feb. 1856.
p. 654. Annual return of Elijah Padget. 25 Feb. 1856.

Scarborough, Noah
pp. 176-7. Bond of Hardy F. Scarborough as guardian
of Francis (Frances) Scarborough, minor heir of Noah
Scarborough, dec'd. Bondsmen: E. E. Glover and John
F. Fisher. 18 Nov. 1854.

Sharp, James P.
Will of James P. Sharp *, Randolph County, Ga.
Wife: Judith H. Sharp
Children: Robert J. Sharp
Sarah S. Sharp
Roxanna E. Jones
James T. Sharp (youngest child)
Excrs: Judith H. Sharp and Robert J. Sharp
Wit: William Y. Barden, W. L. Floyd, H. W. Edwards.
Date: 10 Apr. 1853.
Recorded: 7 Nov. 1853, Randolph Co., Ga.
14 Apr. 1854, Barbour Co., Ala.

Shipman, James
p. 35. Account of sale of slaves, James L. Shipman,
admr. 22 May 1854.
p. 86. Return of Commissioners appointed to divide
slaves report that the balance of the undivided slaves
cannot be equally distributed without a sale.
15 Mar. 1854.
p. 219. Petition of James L. and Alexander Shipman,
admrs., to sell land for division to heirs.
pp. 220-2. List of heirs:
Catherine, wife of Jonathan Lampley
Alexander Shipman
Apaline, wife of Benjamin Lampley, Pike Co.
James L. Shipman
Eliza Shipman, widow of the dec'd.
Lucy, wife of Harvey A. McRae

* Recorded: CONVEYANCE RECORDS BOOK "L". pp. 179-81.

George Shipman
Lewis Shipman
Jesse Shipman, minor
Benjamin F. Shipman, minor
24 Aug. 1854.
p. 223. Authorized to sell land situated in Barbour
and Pike Counties. 24 Aug. 1854.
pp. 301-2. Return of sale of real estate in Barbour
and Pike Counties. 1 Jan. 1855.

Short, William
pp. 568-9. Return of C. F. Gerke, admr. 5 Nov. 1855.
p. 569. Petition for final settlement. The only heir
of William Short is Richard V. Short, a brother of the
dec'd., residing in Barbour County.
p. 570. Final settlement to Richard V. Short.
17 Dec. 1855.

Shorter, R. C.
pp. 495-6. Return of sale of real estate and slaves, Eli
S. Shorter, excr. 5 Nov. 1855.
pp. 556-7. Return of Eli S. Shorter. 7 Nov. 1855.
p. 558. Heirs of the estate:
    Mary B. Shorter, the widow
    John Gill Shorter
    Sarah E., widow of James L. Hunter
    Eli S. Shorter
    Mary B., wife of W. H. Thornton
    Henry R. Shorter
    Reubin F. C. Kolb, son of David C. and Emily F.
                Kolb, dec'd.
    Minor children of Martha G. McLeroy, dec'd., wife
                of W. H. McLeroy, New Orleans:
        Emily McLeroy   Mary McLeroy
        John McLeroy   Sarah McLeroy
    Laura W., wife of Thomas W. Cowles, Montgomery
    Sons of Reubin C. Shorter, Jr., dec'd.:
        James B. Shorter
        Reubin C. Shorter
    Caroline Shorter, widow of Ruebin C. Shorter,Jr.
7 Nov. 1855.

Simpson, minors
p. 488. Bond of Eli S. Shorter as guardian of:
    John D. T. Simpson
minor under the age of 14 years. Bondsman: John Gill
Shorter. 26 Oct. 1855.
p. 489. ibid, Virginia Simpson
p. 669. Return of Eli S. Shorter, guardian.
26 Jan. 1856.

Sinquefield Asa
pp. 375-6. Petition of A. L. Gaston, admr., for an

order to declare the estate of Asa Sinquefield insolvent. 20 Oct. 1854.
pp. 377-8. Notices to creditors that the estate is
declared insolvent. 11 Dec. 1855.
pp. 581-4. Final settlement of A. L. Gaston, admr.,
with creditors, the estate heretofore declared
insolvent. 14 Jan. 1856.

Slack, Archibald C.
pp. 256-9. Final return of William A. Andrews, admr.
20 Oct. 1854.
p. 259-62. Heirs:
Elizabeth, a sister, wife of John Bently, resides
in Tallapoosa or Chambers Co., Ala.
J. B. Slack, a brother
David G. Slack, a brother
Rhoda Andrews, dec'd., her heirs are:
Malinda Benton, Thomas Co., Ga.
W. A. Andrews. Barbour Co.
C. J. M. Andrews
Heirs of Anna Slack, a sister, dec'd., to-wit:
John Slack
Thomas Slack
Jacob Slack, Cherkee Co., Miss.
Rhoda, wife of Samuel G. Wheatly, Wilks Co., Ga.
Selina, wife of Erastus Holland, Russell Co., Ala.
Hannah, wife of John Croner, Indiana
11 Dec. 1854.

Slack, John
p. 277. Petition of Mary Ann Slack, widow of John
Slack, and guardian of:
Jesse Slack, age 20
Frances Slack, age 14
John Slack, age 6
to sell slaves belonging to the minors and heirs of
the estate, to-wit:
James Slack, age 21
Letty Ann, wife of George Reynolds, who sold their
interest to Mary Ann Slack.
13 Nov. 1854.
p. 278. Authorized to sell slaves. 11 Dec. 1854.

Spear, David
pp. 86-7. Annual return of William Blair, guardian of
William Spear, minor. 17 Mar. 1854.
p. 115. Resignation of William Blair as guardian.
23 Sept. 1854.
p. 172. Bond of Henry G. Spear as guardian of William
Spear, minor. Bondsmen: R. S. Wright and M. H. Streeter.
24 Oct. 1854.
pp. 254-6. Final settlement of William Blair with
Henry G. Spear, the present guardian of William Spear.
9 Oct. 1854.

pp. 521-3. Petition Henry G. Spear, guardian of
William Spear, minor heir of David Spear, to sell land
to invest proceeds on personal property.
17 Aug. 1855.
p. 575. Return of sale of land. 14 Jan. 1856.
p. 697. Return of Henry G. Spear, guardian.
29 Feb. 1856.

Stanley, Lewis
pp. 478-9. Will of Lewis Stanley
Wife: Elizabeth J. Stanley
Her children: John Walker Stanley
Parmenas Berean Stanley
Sarah Wilkinson Stanley
Oldest children:
Leven Alatha A. Tinsley *
James G. Stanley
William L. Stanley
Sherwood L. Stanley
William M. Stanley
Frances E. Chitwood
Emily E. Millsap
Excrs: Elizabeth J. Stanley and son-in-law,
Templeton C. Millsap
Wit: Joseph A. Holland, William F. Rogers and
Gideon Y. Thompson.
Date: 19 June 1855.
Recorded: 8 Oct. 1855.
p. 480. Henry D. Clayton appointed ad Litem of:
John W. Stanley
Parmenas B. Stanley
Sarah W. Stanley
10 Sept. 1855.
p. 484. Bond of Temple (Templeton?) C. Millsap and
Elizabeth Stanley as excrs. of the will of Lewis Stanley.
Bondsmen: John W. Clark, Whit Clark and William Ivy.
16 Oct. 1855.
pp. 491-3. Inventory and appraisal of personal property
by commissioners, T. C. Millsap, admr. 6 Nov. 1855.

Stembridge, Henry H. B. **
p. 29. Return of Samuel McBride, guardian of:
John A. Stembridge
Sarah E. Stembridge
24 Apr. 1854.
pp. 77-8. ibid, 13 Mar. 1854.
pp. 382-4. ibid, 12 Feb. 1855.
p. 629. ibid, 11 Feb. 1856.
pp. 701-2. ibid, 11 Feb. 1856.

* Also listed as A. A. Tinsley. See Estate of Charles Tinsley.
** ABSTRACTS OF WILLS & ESTATES II: Henry R. M. Stembridge,
Crawford County, Ga.

Stewart, Norman
      p. 105. Bond as admx. of Jane Stewart, widow of Norman Stewart, dec'd. Bondsmen: Alexander Stewart, Daniel L. Stewart and John L. Stewart. 13 Sept. 1854.
      pp. 118-9. Inventory and appraisal of the estate by commissioners. 5 Oct. 1854.

Stovall, George W.
      pp. 428-30. Annual return of Thomas J. Roquemore, guardian of:
            Cicero Stovall
            George Stovall
            Mary Stovall
      27 Apr. 1855.
      p. 575. Return of sales of slaves belonging to Mary Stovall, minor. 29 Nov. 1855.

Stringer, James A.
      p. 192. Bond as guardian of Richard H. Fryer for:
         Emma L. Stringer, under the age of 14 years, minor heir of James A. Stringer, dec'd. Bondsmen: Mathew Fenn, G. W. Fryer, Seth Mabrey and H. D. Clayton. 25 Nov. 1854.
      p. 193. Bond of Richard H. Fryer as admr. of the estate of James A. Stringer, Jr., dec'd. Bondsmen same as above.
      25 Nov. 1854.
      p. 214. Petition of Jesse Batts, admr., to divide property. Heirs are:
            Sarah A. Stringer, relict of dec'd.
            Emma Stringer, minor
            Lilly Stringer, minor
            James A. Stringer, minor
      All minors under the age of ten years, the last two children have since died. 25 Oct. 1854.
      p. 263. Petition of Jesse Batts, admr., to sell personal property, except slaves, for division to heirs and to pay debts of the estate. 13 Nov. 1854.
      p. 416. Supplementary inventory and appraisal of the real and personal estate by commissioners. 22 July 1854.
      pp. 450-1. Petition of Richard H. Fryer, guardian of Emma Stringer, to sell land to invest proceeds in bonds of exchange at interest as security. D. M. Seals appointed guardian ad Litem of minor. 31 July 1855. Authorized to sell land. 3 Sept. 1855.

Stringer, Lilly G.
      p. 192. Bond of Richard H. Fryer as admr. of the estate of Lilly G. Stringer, dec'd. Bondsmen: Mathew Fenn, G. W. Fryer, Seth Mabrey and Henry D. Clayton. 25 Nov. 1854.

Tarver, Benjamin H.
      p. 305. Bond of Asa T. Miller as admr. of the estate

of B. H. Tarver, dec'd. Bondsmen: Isham C. Browder
and David Slone. 1 Jan. 1855.

Thomas, Eli
      p. 181. Supplemental inventory of the estate by
Jonathan Thomas, admr. 24 July 1854.
      pp. 406-7. Supplemental inventory and return of
Jonathan Thomas, guardian of:
          Mary P. Thomas   Zacheriah T. Thomas
          George H. Thomas
      2 Apr. 1855.

Thompson, Robert
      p. 373. Bond of Seth Mabrey as admr. de Bonis non of
the estate of Robert Thompson. Bondsman: Francis Johns.
5 March 1855.
      p. 504. Adam C. Thompson, minor heir of Robert Thomp-
son, over the age of 14 years, selects his mother,
Rhoda Graves, as his guardian. 15 Nov. 1855.
      p. 504. Bond of Rhoda Graves as guardian of Adam C.
Thompson. Bondsman: Adam Grubbs. 15 Nov. 1855.

Thornton, John
      p. 432. Annual return of W. H. Thornton, guardian of:
          Joseph B. Thornton
      1 May 1855.
      p. 433. Final settlement of W. H. Thornton, guardian
of Edward Q. Thornton. He has arrived at the age of
21 years. 1 May 1855.

Trammell, James J.
      p. 440. Bond of Daniel M. Trammell as guardian of:
          John H. Trammell
      Bondsmen: Josiah M. Carr and L. C. Carr.
      8 Sept. 1855.
      p. 444. Bond as guardian of Penelope N. Cannon for:
          Ann P. J. Trammell
      Bondsmen: Duncan G. Campbell and Jonathan Thomas.
      22 Aug. 1855.
      p. 445. ibid, Eliza J. Trammell
      pp. 686-7. Return of Daniel M. Trammell, guardian.
15 Feb. 1856.

Truetlin, G. E. (Gabriel)
      p. 29. Return of John L. Cleckley, admr. of the
estate of Gabriel E. Truetlin. 2 May 1854.
      p. 92. Return of John L. Cleckley, guardian of:
          Sarah Truetlin
          Mary A. Truetlin
          Cornelia Truetlin
          Julia Truetlin
          Caroline V. Berry, late Truetlin
      2 May 1854.
      p. 415. Return of John L. Cleckley, admr. of the

estate of Mary Ann Truetlin, dec'd. 8 June 1855.
p. 416. Return of John L. Cleckley, admr. of the
estate of Sarah Truetlin, dec'd. 8 June 1855.
p. 416. Return of John L. Cleckley, guardian of
Cornelia and Julia Truetlin. 8 June 1855.
p. 670. ibid, 28 Jan. 1856.

Truetlin, Sarah
p. 330. Petition of John L. Cleckley, admr., to
divide slaves of the estate of Sarah Truetlin, dec'd.,
among her sisters and brother:
John Truetlin
Celista, wife of A. W. Barnett
Caroline, wife of Thomas Berry
Cornelia Truetlin
Julia Truetlin
20 Feb. 1855.
p. 416. Return of John L. Cleckley, admr. 8 June 1855.

Turk, James L.
pp. 223-4. Final return of P. P. Hodges, guardian of
George W. Turk
who has now arrived at the age of 21 years.
10 July 1854.

Turner, minors
p. 415. Return of Noel W. Turner, guardian of:
John R. and Caroline E. Turner
4 June 1855.
p. 630. ibid, 1 Feb. 1856.

Upshaw, James R.
pp. 146-7. List of vouchers and accounts of the estate
of James R. Upshaw, William, T. Upshaw, admr.
pp. 148-9. Final settlement to:
Maria G. Upshaw, widow of dec'd.
Eugenia Upshaw, minor dau. of dec'd.
3 May 1854.
pp. 161-3. Petition of William T. Upshaw, guardian of
Eugenia Upshaw, to sell personal property and invest
the proceeds in slaves. 19 June 1854.
p. 417. Bond of Leroy Upshaw as guardian of Eugenia
Upshaw. Bondsmen: John W. Brown and Maria G. Upshaw.
8 June 1855.

Vann, Isaac
p. 546. Final settlement of Sarah Vann, guardian,
with her ward, Joseph L. Vann, son of Isaac Vann,
dec'd., who has now attained his majority.
24 Dec. 1855.

Warren, Burris
p. 62. Annual return of Lucinda Warren, guardian of:

Burris Warren, (Jr.)
Bates Warren
Georgianna Warren
28 Feb. 1854.
pp. 452-3. Return of Thomas S. Smart, guardian of:
Monroe Warren
9 June 1855.
p. 649. Return of Gilbert McCall, agent for Lucinda
Warren and guardian of Burris, Bates and Georgeanna
Warren. 28 Feb. 1856.

Warren, Edward
p. 50. Annual settlement of Nancy and William Loveless, guardians of Lucina (Lucinda) Warren.
p. 51. Return of Thomas E. Warren, guardian of:
Jackson Warren and Adaline Warren
31 Jan. 1854.
p. 52. Return of John W. Clark, guardian of:
Sarah A. Warren
11 Feb. 1854.
p. 53. Final settlement for America Warren, now the
wife of Henry C. Ward. 10 Feb. 1854.
p. 54. Return of Lovard Lee, Jr., guardian of:
Elvira Loveless
E. K. P. Warren
13 Feb. 1854.
p. 177. Bond of Lovard Lee, Jr., as guardian of:
Elvira Loveless and E. K. P. Warren
Bondsmen: William Loveless, Nancy Loveless and
William King. 18 Nov. 1854.
pp. 331-2. Final settlement of Thomas E. Warren,
guardian of Jackson L. and Adeline Warren, minors.
Henry D. Clayton appointed guardian ad Litem of
minors. 3 Feb. 1855.
p. 435. Bond of Thomas E. Warren as guardian of
Jackson L. Warren. Bondsmen: Nancy Loveless, William
Loveless and Lovard Lee, Jr. 13 Aug. 1855.
pp. 435-6. ibid, Adeline Warren
pp. 687-8 Return of Loveard Lee, Jr., guardian of
E. K. P. Warren. 12 Feb. 1856.
p. 688. ibid, Elivra Loveless
pp. 695-6. Return of John W. Clark, guardian of
Sarah Warren. R. J. Yarrington appointed guardian
ad Litem. 8 Mar. 1856.

Warren, Rebecca
p. 28. Bond of Joel D. Warren as admr. of the estate
of Rebecca Warren. Bondsmen: W. W. Johnston and
Hart Collins. 12 June 1854.
p. 30. Appraisal of personal property, J. D. Warren,
admr. 16 June 1854.
p. 31. Petition of Joel D. Warren to sell personal
property for payment of debts. Heirs listed below.
16 June 1854.

pp. 212-3. Return of sale of personal property, Joel
D. Warren, admr. 17 Oct. 1854.
p. 468. Return of Joel D. Warren. 9 Aug. 1855.
pp. 469-71. Final settlement to:
    Joel D. Warren, a son
    Nancy Anglin, a dau. (wife of Franklin Anglin)
    James E. Warren, a son, residing in Texas
    Milly, a dau., wife of John M. Lampley
    Rebecca *, gr-dau., wife of James L. Beasley
    Thomas A. Efurd, gr-son *
    Giles C. Efurd, gr-son *
    Children of Martha Herring, dec'd.:
        Richard H. Herring, gr-son
        William W. Herring, gr-son
        Mary A. Herring, gr-dau.
        Nancy A. Herring, gr-dau.
    Rebecca, wife of William Bishop, gr-dau.
    Children of Thomas J. Warren, a son, dec'd.:
        Martha S. Thomas, gr-dau.
        Thomas M. Warren, gr-son
        James E. Warren, gr-son
        Joseph M. Warren, gr-son
  Mary, wife of A. F. Utsey, a dau.
4 Sept. 1855.

Warren, Thomas, Sr.
    pp. 117-8. Petition pf Joel D. Warren, admr., for
division of slaves. Heirs listed below. Rebecca
Warren, relict of Thomas Warren, Sr., died on the
26 May 1854. Commissioners authorized to divide
slaves. 5 June 1854.
    p. 132. Report of commissioners that slaves cannot be
equally divided without a sale. 12 June 1854.
    p. 211. Return of sale of personal property, Joel D.
Warren, admr. 17 Oct. 1854.
    pp. 466-8. Return of Joel D. Warren. 9 Aug. 1855.
Final settlement to:
    Nancy, wife of Franklin Anglin
    Rebecca, wife of James T. Beasley
    Thomas A. Efurd
    Giles C. Efurd
    Richard H. Herring
    William W. Herring
    Mary A. Herring
    Nancy A. Herring
9 Aug. 1855.

Warren, Thomas J.
    p. 609. Bond of William Bishop as guardian of:
    Susan Warren, minor
Bondsmen: Joseph C. Russell and James B. Bishop.
5 Feb. 1856.

* Rebecca Beasley, Thomas A. and Giles C. Efurd were children
of Giles C. Efurd (Sr.) and _____ Warren.

pp. 609-10. ibid, James Warren
pp. 676-7. Return of Sarah Warren, guardian of:
    Thomas M. and Joel Warren
minor heirs of Thomas J. Warren, dec'd.
4 Feb. 1856.
pp. 679-80. Final settlement of Sarah Warren, guardian
of James E. Warren, with the present guardian, William
Bishop. 7 Feb. 1856.
pp. 681-2. ibid, Susan Warren
p. 700. Bond of Thomas C. Helms, in right of his wife,
Sarah, late Sarah Warren, as guardian of Thomas Warren.
Bondsmen: Hart Collins and W. W. Helms. 22 Mar. 1856.

Watson, Peter
        pp. 79-80. Final return of Elizabeth Watson, guardian
        of:
            John J. Watson
            James F. M. Watson
            Peter Watson
            Daniel G. Watson
            Jesse Z. Watson
            Nathan C. Watson
            Rebecca Paul
        now of the age of 21 years. 18 Mar. 1854.

Weathers, Samuel
        p. 39. Bond of William Weathers and Jane Weathers as
        admrs. of the estate of Samuel Weathers, dec'd. Bonds-
        men: Theophilus Bryan and M. A. Browder. 26 June 1854.
        pp. 186-8. Inventory and appraisal of personal property
        by commissioners. 14 Aug. 1854.
        p. 200. Resignation of W. H. Sterns and Jane Sterns as
        admrs. of the estate. Said Jane Sterns being the widow
        of Samuel Weathers. 8 Dec. 1854.
        p. 215. Petition of William Weathers and Wilson Sterns,
        in right of his wife, Jane Sterns, late Weathers, to
        sell perishable property to pay debts of the estate.
        Authorized to sell same. 6 Nov. 1854.
        p. 315. Bond of William Weathers as admr. of the estate.
        Bondsmen: Theophilus Bryan and Milton A. Browder.
        12 Feb. 1855.
        pp. 356-7. Petition of Jane Sterns, wife of Wilson H.
        Sterns, and widow of Samuel Weathers, for her dower,
        which is land in Barbour County, relinquishing a portion
        which was sold to William Weathers. Samuel Weathers left
        no heirs except the following sisters and brothers:
            William Weathers
            Amy (or Anna), wife of John Sheppard
            Sally, wife of William Thomas
            Elizabeth, wife of Anderson McNeill
            Solomon Weathers, Macon County, Alabama
            Patsey, wife of Samuel Weathers, non resident

Peggy, wife of Jonathan Woodall, non resident
Polly, wife of Wilson Rhea, non resident
13 Nov. 1854.
p. 358. Commissioners appointed to set off dower
claims. 8 Jan. 1855.
pp. 359-60. Report of commissioners on dower claim.
Ordered by court that dower be allotted to petitioner.
8 Jan. 1855.
pp. 533-4. Petition of William Weathers, admr., to
sell land for division to heirs, the same as above
with the exception of:
    Annie (or Anna), wife of John Sheppard
    Margaret, wife of Jonathan Woodall
    Patsy, wife of Samuel Weathers, Pike Co., Ala.
    Children of Polly Ray, dec'd., non residents,
           names not known except Martha Harris,
           Montgomery County, Ala.
p. 335. Admr. authorized to sell land, subject to
widow's dower. 29 Oct. 1855.
p. 542. Petition of William Weathers, admr., to sell
slaves for equal division to heirs. 29 Oct. 1855.
pp. 693-4. Return of William Weathers, admr.
11 Feb. 1856.

Whitehurst, Asa
p. 369. Application for letters of administration for
the estate of Asa Whitehurst by James Shanks, Sr.,
who states that Levi Whitehurst, dec'd., in his will
left a slave to Asa Whitehurst, a son, dec'd. The
surviving heir is George Ann Whitehurst, a minor
living in Pike County, Ala.
p. 370. Ordered by court that James Shanks, Sr.,
be appointed admr. of the estate of Asa Whitehurst.
3 Mar. 1855.
p. 374. Bond of James Shanks, Sr., as admr. Bondsmen: George Shanks and Nathan Minshew. 7 Mar. 1855.

Whitehurst, Levi
pp. 337-8. Annual return of Mary B. Whitehurst, excr.
Heirs are:
    Cynthia, wife of James Wood, Sumpter Co., Ala.
    Asa Whitehurst, over age 21, East Florida
    Mary Ann Whitehurst, minor, Barbour Co., Ala.
Henry D. Clayton appointed guardian ad Litem of
minor heir. 15 Aug. 1854.
pp. 637-8. Return of Mary B. Whitehurst, excr.
15 Jan. 1856.

Williams, Austin
pp. 365-9. Annual return of Benjamin F. Petty, admr.
Heirs are:
    Mary O. Williams, widow of the dec'd.
    Mary Jane, wife of Charles Pratt

John L. Williams, minor
Henry D. Clayton appointed guardian ad Litem of minor heir. 12 Jan. 1855.

Williams, Butler
p. 651. Return of J. J. Dickson, guardian of:
Luna A. Dickson
minor heir of Butler Williams, dec'd., from Samuel L. Williams and B. F. Williams, excrs. of the estate of Butler Williams. 8 Mar. 1856.

Williams, Osborn J.
pp. 101-2. Bond of Sophia Williams, widow of Osborn J. Williams, as admx. of the estate. Bondsmen: James Ventress, Buckner Williams and Thomas Ventress. 18 July 1854.
pp. 149-55. Inventory and appraisal of the estate by commissioners. 15 Aug. 1854.
p. 215. Petition of Sophia Williams, admx., to divide slaves. Heirs are:
Sophia Williams, widow of dec'd.
Ann, wife of Augustus L. Oliver
James Williams, minor, under the age of 14 years
Commissioners authorized to divide slaves.
4 Nov. 1854.
p. 270. Petition of Sophia Williams, admx., to sell personal property, except slaves, for division among heirs and to pay debts of the estate. Authorized to sell property. 24 Nov. 1854.
p. 286. Report of commissioners on division of slaves. 10 Nov. 1854.
pp. 308-9. Petition of Sophia Williams, admx., to sell land for equal division to heirs. The real estate is the Tavern House and lots in the town of Clayton.
p. 310. Authorized to sell property. 20 Nov. 1854.
pp. 374-5. Return of Sophia Williams, admx., on the sale of real and personal property. 10 Mar. 1855.

Williams, Owen G.
p. 639. Final return of Jacob Parmer, guardian of:
E. C. (Elender Williams
minor heir of Owen G. Williams, with Thomas S. Kettler, of Butler Co., with the present guardian. Thomas S. Kettler, present guardian, asks that the estate be removed to Butler County. 14 Jan. 1856.

Williams, William H., Dr.
p. 201. Resignation of Mrs. M. A. Williams, widow of William H. Williams, as admx. of her husband's estate.
p. 201. Bond of Jere N. Williams as admr. Bondsmen: John C. McNeill and J. S. Williams. 9 Dec. 1854.
p. 278. Inventory and appraisal by commissioners. 11 Dec. 1854.

p. 331. Supplemental appraisal by commissioners of
a lot in the town of Abbeville, Henry Co., Ala.
20 Feb. 1855.
p. 342. Petition of Jere N. Williams, admr., to sell
personal property, except slaves, for payment of
debts. Authorized to sell property.
13 Dec. 1854.
pp. 371-3. Return of Jere N. Williams on the sales
of perishable property. 5 Mar. 1855.

Wood, Jesse, minor
     p. 342. Return of W. E. Price, guardian of:
        Jesse Wood, minor
     17 Oct. 1854.

Abney, William, 17
Adams, Ann, 16
, Caroline, 16
, Elias, 16
, Elizabeth, 16
, Henry, 2
, Jefferson, 16
, Sarah, 16
Allen, Micajah, 66
Allison, Reubin, 71
Anders, William A., 92
Anderson, Allice, 51
, C. B., 50
, Charles, 51
, David, 69
, G. J., 69
, G. W., 69
, George, 22
, J. T., 69
, John (J.), 22, 69
, Margaret, 22, 69
, Margaret K., 69
, Mary, 22, 69
, Mary Ann, 22, 69
, Morgan, 69
, Russell, 22, 69
, S. P., 69
, Samuel, 22, 69
, Thomas, 51
Andrews, C. J. M., 12, 70, 92
, Rhoda, 92
, William A., 12, 60, 92
Anglin, Andrew J., 51
, Ann Texas, 51
, Francis, 47
, Franklin, 47, 51, 98
, Joseph, 52
, Nancy, 47, 98
, Thomas W., 51
, Victoria, 51
Arrington, Amos, 1
, Elisha, 1, 52
, Elizabeth, 67
, Francis, 1
, Jeremiah, 1
, William, 1
Averett, Jackson, 25, 74
, Mary, 25, 74
Ayers, Ann Eliza, 73
, Eliza, 24
, James (B.), 24, 73
Baggett, Wiley, 39
Baker, Enos H., 2
, F. E., 1, 34

Baker, Franklin E., 34, 65
, H. W., 27
, James, 1, 2, 52
, Jarrett, 2
, Lydia, 1. 2, 52
, Margaret, 1, 52
, Mathew, 2
, Peggy, 2
, Robert, 2
, Thomas E., 1
, William, 1, 2
, Winney, 1, 2, 52
Ball, Edward, 23
Ballard, William L., 52
Barbour, Jaret P., 2
, Sarah, 2
Barden, William Y., 90
Barham, William A., 44
Barker, George W., 77
Barkley, William, 74
Barnes, Mary A. S., 58
Barnett, A. W., Dr., 44, 96
, Celista, 44, 96
, James E., 59, 73
, James R., 12
, Julius C., 2, 52
, Lucy, 73
, Mary A., 2, 52
, Mary O., 2, 52
, Samuel, 23
, Sarah V., 2, 52
, Thomas J., 2, 52
, William E., 71
Barron, B. A., 46
, Benjamin A., 1
Bass, Everett, 53
, Fanny, 53
, Josiah, 53
, Mary Jane, 52, 53
, Sarah Elizabeth, 53
, Uriah, 53
, Willis, 52, 53
Bates, Wilson M., 76
Batts, Jesse, 20, 40, 94
Baxter, Mary, Mrs., 49
, Thomas F., 8, 53
Beasley, James L., 48, 98
, Rebecca, 48, 98
Beauchamp, Eliza J., 3
, Eliza Jane, 53
, Green, 3, 53
, Henry W., 3, 53
, Joseph, 3, 53
, Richard K., 3, 53

Beauchamp, Thomas H., 3
Beck, Basheba, 24, 73
    , J. B., 24
    , John S., 73
Beckham, Burrell, 3
    , Rachel, 3
Beckman, Francis M., 10
    , Manerva W., 10
Bellette, Ella, 3
    , James, 3
    , Famelia F., 3
Bennett, Alexander, 4
    , Benjamin C., 4, 54
    , Eli F., 3, 4, 54
    , Emily, 5, 54
    , James A., 3, 54
    , Julia Ann, 4, 54
    , Mary A., 4
    , Nancy, 3, 53
    , Nevel, 4, 53
    , Ryan, 5, 54
    , Silas (A.), 4, 53
    , Thomas (B.), 53
    , W. A., 4
    , William A., 3, 54
Bently, Elizabeth, 92
    , John, 92
Benton, Malinda, 92
    , Mary, 4
Berry, Caroline, 44, 95, 96
    , Thomas, 44, 96
Bethune, Cornelia, 4, 5
    , Elizabeth S. 4
    , John S., 4, 5, 43
    , Mary R., 4
    , Nancy, 43
    , Robert A., 4
    , Sarah V., 4
    , Virginia, 5
    , William J., 4, 5
Beverly, Anne E., 5, 54
    , Christian (N.), 5, 54
    , Daniel G., 5, 54
    , Mary (J.), 5, 54
    , William (N.), 5, 53
Bigham, James, 19, 78
Birdsong, Elizabeth T., 65
    , Josephine, 65
    , Martha Ann, 65
    , William H., 65
Bishop, B. D., 5
    , Dixon H., 54, 67
    , Dixon H. L., 5
    , J. B., 6
    , James B., 5, 54, 98

Bishop, Nancy, 5
    , Rebecca, 47, 98
    , Wesley, 5. 54
    , William, 5, 47, 54,
                98, 99
Bizzell, Casandra, 14, 62
    , Curtis J., 14
    , Harrison F., 54
    , Henry B., 14, 62
    , Henry H., 14
    , Henry N., 49, 54
    , James C., 62
    , Jennett, 14
    , Mary J., 62
    , W. A., 6, 54
    , William A., 54, 87
Blair, Elizabeth, 5, 54
    , Michael W., 22
    , William, 5, 38, 54, 92
Bledsoe, John W., 20, 44
Bludworth, Elizabeth A., 54, 55
    , Florence, 55
    , Patrick, 54, 66
Bolton, Amanda, 55
    , Elijah, 55
Bostick, Eli, 24
Boswell, W. H., 76
Bowden, Lewis, 9
Bowers, Henry C., 49
Boylston, Eleanor, 41
    , Joseph C., 41
Branch, Charles J., 19
    , Nancy, 19
Brandon, A. P., 10
Bridges, Daniel B., 82
Britt, Asa F., 6
    , Catherine V., 6
    , Elizabeth, 6
    , Ira, 61
    , John T., 6
    , Mathew T., 6
    , Moses, 6
    , Sarah, 6
    , William R., 6
Broach, William, 13, 61
Browder, I. C. 19, 57
    , Isham C., 76, 95
    , M. A., 99
Brown, John W., 96
    , L. H., 90
    , Nancy, 74
Bryan, Amanda, 55, 56
    , Benjamin, 56
    , Benjamin L., 55
    , Eliza Ann, 55, 56

Bryan, George, 55
    , Green (L.), 55, 56
    , James, 55, 56
    , John C., 6, 45, 55
    , Neel, 56
    , Sarah, 55
    , Susan, 56
    , Theophilus, 99
    , William, 6
    , William M., 6, 55
    , William N., 55
Buford, Jefferson, 50
Bullard, James, 3
Bullock, E. C., 11
    , Edward C., 13, 24, 52, 74, 82

Bush, C. D., 41, 42
    , Charles D., 7, 56
    , Council, 5, 49, 54
    , D. A., 15
    , David A., 15
    , Frances J., 7, 56
    , Hilliard H., 56
    , Julia, 15
    , Lucinda, 7, 8, 56
    , Mary A., 56
    , Mary R., 7
    , Moses E., 7, 56
    , Rebecca, 5, 54
    , Ruth C., 7
    , Salina B., 56
    , Selina B., 6, 7
    , W. G., 7
    , William G., 7, 41, 42, 56
    , William M., 56
    , Zacheriah, 7, 56
Butt, R. L., 71
Byrd, Edward, 49
Cadenhead, Ann E., 57, 72, 73
    , Eliz. 50
    , Isaac, 57
    , James, 57, 73
    , Sarah E., 75
    , Sarah S., 57, 72
Calaway, Daniel, 31
Cameron, Christian, 82
    , Hugh, 75
    , John, 82
Campbell, Ann, 8
    , Cathy Ann, 8
    , Cynthia Ann, 8
    , Duncan, 8, 95
    , Joab, 8

Campbell, Mary Ann, 8
    , Nancy, 8
    , Neely, 8
Cannon, Penelope N., 43, 95
    , S. R., 43
    , Simeon, 43
Cargile, Thomas, 38
Carmichael, Archibald, 11, 83
Carnes, Eliza J., Mrs., 49
Carr, James Madison, 9
    , Josiah M., 9, 95
    , L. C., 96
    , Letitia Caroline, 9
    , Louisa C., 9
    , Thomas J., 9
Casey, Cloe, 71
    , Henry, 71
Cato, Lewis L., 35
Causey, Cullen, 57
    , D. R., 9
    , Greenberry, 57
    , James L., 58
    , James S., 9
    , Joseph, 58
    , Joseph W., 9
    , Lewellen, 58
    , Phillip B., 9
    , Randerson, (Dr.), 9, 58
    , Wiley, 58
    , William, 58
Cawthorn, Charity J., 10, 58
    , Josiah A. J., 10, 58
    , Martha, 10, 58
    , Sarah E., 10, 58
    , Sidney F., 10
    , Simeon S., 10
    , Simon, 58
    , Stephen, 9
    , William W., 10, 58
Chambers, I. H., 57
    , Isaac H., 8
Chaney, Milbry, 59
Chesnut, Michael, 76
Chisholm, Janett, 81
    , Roderick C., 81
Chitwood, Frances E., 93
Clark, J. W., 59
    , James, 50
    , John W., 15, 22, 27, 47, 50, 51, 79, 80, 93, 97
    , Whit, 93
    , Whitfield, 19, 22, 50 56, 90

Clayton, H. D., 60, 64, 76, 94
        , Henry D., 6, 20, 21, 22,
            35, 36, 37, 44, 46,
            51, 52, 55, 68, 81,
            87, 89, 90, 93
Cleckley, Adison D., 44
        , John L. 44, 96
Clements, Jesse, 88
Clemons, Jesse, 88
        , Suprina, 88
Cobb, Augustus M. C., 10
        , Cary L., 10
        , Harriett W. S., 10
        , Jesse C., 10
        , John L., 10
        , Joshua A., 10
        , Mary J., 10
        , Nancy S.S.S., 10
        , Susan E., 10
        , Walter S. G., 10
        , Walton F. M., 10
        , William H. C., 10
Cole, Amazon, 11
        , Calista A., 11
        , D. S., 67
        , Wealthy, 11
Coleman, Benjamin F., 11, 59
        , Charles D., 11, 59
        , Jesse B., 59
        , Joseph R., 11
        , Mary Emma, 11, 59
        , William T., 11, 59
Collins, Hart, 97, 99
        , Hartwell, 50
        , M., 26, 27
        , Wilson, 49
Comer, John F., 23, 79
Conner, George D., 17
Cooper, Mary, 55
        , William, 55
Cotton, Missouri F., 11
Couch, Julia E., 4
        , William, 4
Covington, B. A., 74
        , Benjamin, 25
        , S. J., 74
        , Sarah, 25
Cowan, W. L., 17
        , William L., 24
Cowart, Eliza M., 60
        , Susan M., 60
        , W., 40
        , William J., 60

Cowen, William L., 71
        , William R., Judge, 3
Cowles, Laura W., 91
        , Thomas W., 91
Cox, Moses, 43, 54
        , William, 44
Crawford, Alex. Penn, 60
        , Cassandra A., 11, 60
        , Ella Roberta, 60
        , Virgil, 60
        , Virginia Penn, 60
Creech, David, 60
        , Francis, 60
        , Nancy A., 39
        , Sion, 39
        , Wesley, 60
        , Wiliam C., 12
Crews, Arthur, 7, 22
        , J. E., 56
        , John E., 50, 64
        , W. B., 7, 22, 52, 64
Croly, Mary, 18
        , Sarah, 18
Croner, Hannah, 92
        , John, 92
Crowder, H. T., 57
        , S., Homer S. 73
Currin, Michael, 85
Daniel, John L., 71
        , Josiah, 25
        , Juliett A., 12
        , Martha, 55, 56
        , Samuel C., 12
        , Sarah E., 12, 60
        , Seaborn, 56
        , Z. J., 38, 48, 83
        , Zodock J., 11
Dansby, Daniel M., 10
        , Isham M., 23
        , Lucinda, 10
Davis, Calvin J., 12
        , Capers, 12
        , David, 50
        , Esther J., 12
        , Frances, 30
        , Frederick, 30, 80
        , Giles, 12
        , Henry M., 12
        , Margaret, Mrs., 12
        , Rebecca E., 12
Dawkins, A. T., 32, 84
        , Mary M., 89
        , Robert H., 89

106

Dew, Lewis, 58
, Sarah, 58
Dick, Mary E., 86
Dickson, J. J., 101
, John J., 61
, Luna A., 61, 101
Dill, Robert, 9, 21, 50
Dixon, Alfred, 13
, Bryant, 13
, Elizabeth, 12
, James W.. 13
, Joseph, 12, 61
, William, 13
Doster, Simeon J., 17
Dubose, Seaborn J., 6, 7, 56
Dudley, J. G., 85
Dykes, James, 55
, Jane, 55
Echols, Clark, 68, 82, 84
, Hester, 84
, Sanders C., 86
Edge, Eli, 61
, Jenny, 61
, Jesse, 61
, Levi, 61
, William, 61
Edwards, H. W., 90
, Nathan B., 58
, Rachael, 58
, W. E., 58
Efurd, Giles C., 48, 61, 66, 98
, Rebecca, 48
, T. C., 66, 67
, Thomas A., 48, 98
, Thomas C., 16
Eidson, Francis, 13, 61
, Mary J., 19
, Oren, 19
Eiland, Absolom, 72
, Allen, 72
Ellis, Ann, 79
, Thomas J., 79
Ethridge, Betsey G., 66
, R. C., 66
Evans, Emanuel, 17
, John, 42
, Mary, 42
Faison, Alex. M., 13
, James D., 13, 61
, Nancy, 13, 61
Farrior, William, 23
Faulk, A. W., 6, 14, 54, 61
, Charlotte, 54
, H. L., 14, 54, 61

Faulk, Henry, Jr., 23, 24
, Henry L., 14, 61
, Isabel A., 62
, J. W., 70
, James E., 62
, James K., 14, 62
, Jane, 54
, John W., 14, 62
, Levi, 74
, M. W., 62
, Mark W., 14
, Martha A. E., 62
, Mary Caroline, 70
, Mary L., 62
, Nancy, 62
, Sarah E., 62
Faulkner, Chesnut, 41
, Sarah J., 41
Feagin, Almira, 10
, Daniel, 14, 62
, George W., 14
, Henry G., 14
, Isaac (B.), 14, 62
, James, 11
, James M., 10, 14, 34, 62
, John R., 14
, Mary, 14
, Mary Ann, 14, 62
, Nancy, 14
, Samuel, 10, 14, 17
, W. J., 14
Fenn, Mathew, 94
Fisher, John F., 90
Flake, Benjamin C., 62
, Eugenia V., 62
, Florida, 62
, Martha J., 62
, William, 62
Flournoy, Catherine, 4
, James, 4, 53
, James A., 3
, Nancy K., 53
, Thomas, 6
Flowers, Abner, 15, 63
, Harral(l), 15, 63
, Levin M., 15
, Rebeca, 15
, Rebecca Ann, 15
, William J., 15
, Wright, 7, 15
Floyd, Charles, 4, 53
, Joseph, 16, 63
, Page, 16, 63
, Sarah, 4

Floyd, Sarah M., 53
      , W. L., 90
Ford, Elcana G., 63
      , Eli N., 63
      , James P., 63
      , William G., 63
Foster, B. F., 35, 88
      Benjamin F., 17
Franklin, Edwin, 10
Fryer, G. W., 94
      , George W., 30
      , R. H., 76
      , Richard H., 94
Fuqua, Jincy, 15
      , John, 15
Furgeson, Robert, 63
Gachet, James E., 23, 70
Gaines, John G., 48
      , Susan Ann E., 48
Gamble, Martha J., 16, 63
Gardner, Eliza Ann, 65
      , Frances H., 65
      , Samuel H., 65
Garland, Hastin, 40
Garrington, R. J., 72
Gary, Frances L., 64
      , Henry D., 64
      , James, 64, 79
      , Sarah J., 64
      , Sarah S., 43
      , W. L., 43
      , William L., 43
Gaston, A. L., 38, 91
Gerke, C. F., 37, 91
Gibson, William H. C., 82
Glenn, A. S., 16
      , Dostheus, 16
      , M. M. 16, 17
Glover, E. E., 90
      , H. Y., 84
      , Rachel, 30, 78
      , Sarah, 84
      , Thomas, 30, 78
Godwin, Ransom, 38, 79
Grantham, Daniel, 22, 69
      , Edward, 22, 69
      , Jesse, 64
      , Jincy, 64
      , John, 22, 69
      , John J., 64
      , Johnson, 22, 69
      , Martha, 64
      , Mary, 22, 64, 69
      , Molsey, 22, 69

Grantham, Prudence, 22, 69
Graves, Caroline T., 17
      , David P., 16
      , Eligah, 16
      , Hardy, 42
      , James, 42
      , Jane, 42
      , John, 16
      , Martha T., 17
      , Mary E., 17
      , Rhoda, 16, 42, 95
      , Sarah J., 17
      , Stephen W., 16
      , Thomas P., 17
      , William L., 17
Green, Ann, 64
      , Gracy A., 55
      , Isabella, 64
      , Jacob, 55
      , Mary, 64
      , Sarah, 64
      , Violetta, 64
      , William L., 64
Greenaway, Jane W., 17
      , Leonora, 17
      , Lucretia A., 17
      , Mary, 17
Grephill, Margaret, 41
      , Wiley, 41
      , Zacheriah, 41
Griffin, Jane, 22, 69
      , Joseph, 22, 69
Griffith, Moses, 17, 64
Griggs, Isabel, 17
      , Mahala, 17
Grubbs, Adam, 18, 67, 95
      , Elizabeth, 17, 65
      , Frances M., 17
      , Green J., 17
      , James, 65
      , James J., 17
      , James M., 17
      , John T., 17, 50
      , Mary, 17, 65
      , Morgan M., 17
      , W. G., 27
      , W. J., 17, 62
      , William T., 17
      , Winn(e)y B., 17, 65
      , Worthy J., 62, 67
Guerrant, Daniel E., 86
Hagler, Jacob, 18
      , Sarah, 18
      , Thomas, 18

Hall, Alexander, 18
  , Charles, 18
  , Daniel, 18
  , Elisha, 18
  , Eliza, 18
  , Emeline, 18
  , Henry, 18
  , John W., 22
  , Margaret, 18
  , Martha, 18
  , Mary, 18, 22
  , Nancy, 18
  , Patience, 18
  , Silas, 18
  , W., 18
Hamrick, Edy M., 65
Hancock, Isiah, 3
Harrelson, Elizabeth, 42
      , John, 42
Hardy, Elizabeth, 84
  , Susanna B., 84
Hargroves, Charity, 19
     , John W., 19
Harp, Allen, 1
  , Emeline, 1
Harper, Ferdinand A.L., 31, 80
  , Henry H., 31
  , Irwin V. O., 31
  , James L. W., 80
  , James W., 31
  , Martha G.G., 31, 80
  , Mary M.C., 30
  , Mary M.O., 80
  , Robert M. (W.), 31, 80
  , Sarah J. (H.), 31, 80
Harris, Martha, 100
  , Thomas, 81
Harwell, Berchet, 19, 65
  , Henry J., 65
  , James H., 19, 65
  , Samuel W., 65
  , Sarah, 74
Hayes, Sarah A., Mrs., 49
Hays, Browder, 58
Head, Thomas J., 1
  , William, 55, 66
Helms, Holly, 59
  , John, 59
  , Sarah, 99
  , Thomas C., 99
  , W. W., 99
Heron, Edward M., 23, 24
Herring, Ann, 48
     , John W., 19

Herring, Martha, 48, 98
  , Mary, 48
  , Mary A., 66, 98
  , Nancy A., 98
  , Polly, 19
  , Richard (H.), 48, 66, 98
  , West, 19
  , William (W.), 48, 66, 98
Hight, Felix, 37
Hightower, Thomas A., 36, 39, 88
Hill, Eliza M. E., 39
  , M. R., 39
  , William D., 39
Hinson, Lemuel, 82
  , Nancy Jane, 67
  , William, 21, 82
Hodges, E. G. 44, 67
  , Elias (G.), 20, 67
  , Elias O., 20
  , George C., 19, 20
  , George D., 19, 20, 67
  , Holiday (H.), 19, 67
  , P. P., 44, 96
  , Pulaski P., 44
  , Richard C., 19
  , Sarah J., 19, 20, 67
Holder, Rosella, 20
Holderly, G. H., 86
  , Joseph B., 86
  , Victor M., 86
Holland, Erastus, 92
  , Joseph A., 86, 93
  , Selina, 92
Holleman, Amanda, 67
  , E. C., 83
  , Eli C., 20, 32, 50
         65, 67
  , Henry (C.), 20, 67
  , Mary (C.), 20, 67
  , Samantha, 65
Holmes, Lewis H., 89
  , Malinda, 89
Holt, A. A., 21
  , Asa, 21
  , Jane M., 21
  , Thomas S., 20
Hood, Bold Robin, 67
  , Daniel S., 67
  , Joshua T., 67
  , Mary Jane, 67
Hoole, Bertram J., 52
  , E. S., 6
Howard, Cornelia, 73
  , R. H., 73

Hudson, G. H., 75
        , Grandbury H., 25
        , Louisiana, 25, 75
Hulin, Elisha, 1
        , Harriet, 1
Hunter, James H., 10
        , James L., 91
        Sarah E., 38, 91
Ivy, John, 19
        , Sarah, 19
Iv(e)y, William, 65, 93
Jacob, Edward, 10
        , Patience L., 10
        , Palistra L., 10
Jackson, Elizabeth, 16, 15, 75
        , Jefferson, 18
        , John W., 25, 75
        , Patience, 18
James, John B., 54
        , Mary, 54
        , Robert, 54
        , Sophrona, 54
Jay, David, 21, 68
        , Elizabeth E., 21, 68
        , John D., 21, 68
Jimmerson, John, 79
Johns, Francis, 95
Johnson, Amanda J., 69
        , Catherine, 21, 68
        , David, 20, 22, 68
        , Elizabeth, 68
        , Felix, 21, 68
        , Frances, 68
        , George, 22
        , George W., 69
        , James, 22, 69
        , James H., 68
        , Jesse, 68
        , John W., 21,22,23,68
                69,70
        , Julia (A,), 21, 68
        , Julian, 21
        , Laura, 68
        , Louisa A., 68
        , Lydia, 68
        , Mary, 22, 69
        , Osborn S., 49
        , Phillip, 43
        , Racnael A., 68
        , Sarah, 69
        , Timothy, 20, 22
        , William W., 20,22,68,82
Johnston, J. D., 34, 86
        , John W., 22, 23

Johnston, Martha F., 4
        , L. F., 4
        , Richard M., 23
        , W. W., 97
Jones, A. E., 2, 5
        , Aerial E., 2
        , Benjamin, 23, 70
        , Derril(1), 23, 80
        , Elender, 23, 70
        , Eugenia, 23
        , James, 4, 53
        , James A., 23
        , Joseph, 23, 70
        , Louisa, 4
        , Louise E., 53
        , Roxanna E., 90
        , Samuel, 23, 70
        , Seaborn, 76
        , Thomas, 23, 70
Jordan, Elbert, 17
        , Mahala, 17
Joyce, Martin H., 38, 85
Kaigler, Rubin, 26
Kenderick, Martha, 14
                , Thomas C., 14
Keneday, W. L., 59
Kenneymore, John C. P., 34
Kennedy, Elizabeth, 85
Kent, Sarah, 38
Ketcham, Ann Eliza, 70
        , Bartley W., 70
        , Benjamin F., 71
        , David H., 70
        , Elizabeth Jane, 70
        , M. D. L., 70
        , Mary Ann, 70
Kettler, Thomas S., 101
Kilpatrick, W. H., 88
Kinchen, Hiram, 84
King, A. H., 34, 57, 83
        , Abi, 72
        , Abner H., 50, 72, 73
        , Anna, 71, 72
        , G. W., 48, 63
        , Harvey, 72
        , Lewis H., 72, 73
        , Levy, 63
        , Marshall, 24, 71
        , Nancy, 24, 71
        , Nancy M., 72, 73
        , Necy S., 24
        , Nicey, 71
        , Richard, 71, 72
        , Robert H., 73

110

King, Sarah, 71, 72
, Sarah Harvey, 71
, Sheppard, 24
, Sheppard W., 71
, Tandy W., 72, 73
, Thomas C., 9
, William, 30, 71, 72, 74
        77, 80, 97
Kolb, David C., 91
, Emily F. 91
, Reubin F. C., 38, 91
Lac(e)y, Elizabeth, 24, 73
, J. F., 24, 73
Lamar, John O., 73
, Lucius, 73
, Martha A., 73
, Sarah E., 73
, Thomas, 73
, William H., 73
Lamb, A. J., 24, 73
, J. G., 24, 73
, Jackson, 74
, Madison, 24, 73
, W. A. B., 73
, William, A. B., 24
Lampley, Apaline, 37, 90
, Benjamin, 37, 90
, Catherine, 90
, Catherine A., 37
, Ira, 61
, J. M., 23, 24, 66, 73
, J. R., 23
, John M., 24, 47, 51, 98
, Jonathan (R.), 37, 90
        Mill(e)y, 47, 98
Lang, Mary, 11
Langford, Edward, 25, 74
, Robert, 25, 74
, Sarah, 25, 74
Lany, Charles D., 52
Lasiter, Jane, 5, 54
, M. M., 54
, Mathew M., 5
, Thomas J., 6, 28, 29, 77
Laws, David, 74
, George, 74
, Henry, 74
, Isaiah, 74
, James (H.), 74
, Jared, 74
, John, 74
, Robert, 74
, William, 74

Lee, Christopher C., 25,26,74
, Columbus, 75
, Eliza Jane, 25
, Jane, 25, 75
, Jesse, 10
, John, 75
, John B., 25
, Lovard, Jr., 25, 47, 74
        75, 98
, Martha, 25, 26
, Martha Ann, 74
, Mary J., 26, 74
, Needham, Jr., 25, 75
, Sally, 25
, Sarah, 26, 75
, Sarah Ann, 74
, Winford, 25, 26, 74
Lelland, Booker J., 86
Lewis, Hanson, 75
, Jane, 75
, Niecy L., 65
, W. M., 71
, William, 75
Ligget, John D., 90
Lightner, Nancy, 5, 54
, T. S., 5
, Thomas S., 54
Lindsey, James, 38
Locke, Jesse, 26, 32, 75, 83
, M. B., 75
, Michael B., 26
, Thomas S., 1, 14, 15, 17,
        18, 26, 27, 31,
        32, 33, 36, 42,
        52, 59, 61, 65,
        66, 75, 79, 80
Long, Betsey, 18
, Charles, 18
Lore, Andrew T., 49
Loveless, Elvira, 46, 47, 97
, Everett, 14, 62
, Nancy, 14, 47, 62, 97
, William, 47, 97
Lovitt, Nancy, 26
Lowe, Robert N. 37
Lowman, Benj. Jos. 27, 76
, Eugene Henry, 27, 76
, James L., 76
, John David, 27, 76
, John J., 76
, John L., 76
, Martha E., 27, 76
, Mary H., 26, 75

Lowman, Mary Susan, 27, 76
, Sarah A. C., 27, 76
, Samuel A., 27, 76
, William G., 27, 76
Mabrey, James W., 18, 53
Seth, 1, 9, 14, 17, 19,
26, 27, 31, 32, 33,
39, 40, 43, 57, 59,
64, 77, 94, 95
Macklrory, Martha G., 38
Mann, Robert, 76
Marley, H. J., 68
, Horatio J., 77
Martin, Andrew J., 28
, Caroline V., 28
, Delila G., 76
, Delphia T., 76
, Elizabeth A., 28
, Francis M., 28, 77
, George W., 28, 77
, Gibson, 39
, Harriet, 28, 77
, Henry F., 17
, James L. C., 28
, John F., 28, 77
, Martha V., 27, 77
, Martin D., 37
, Mary A., 28, 77
, Mary J., 27, 77
, Mathew A., 28
, Penelope A., 27, 76
, Samuel M., 28
, Sarah, 28, 77
, Sarah E., 27, 77
, Sarah J., 28, 77
, Seleta O., 27, 77
, Seleta W., 27, 39
, Thomas W., 28
, Victoria C., 28, 77
, William H., 28, 77
Marshall, Amanda, Mrs., 3
, Thomas P., 38
Mayo, John, 26
McBride, Catherine J., 29
, Eliza, 78
, Eliza Ann, 29
, James P., 29, 78
, John, 78
, Mary A., 29
, Mary Agnes, 29, 78
, Samuel, 29, 39, 78, 93
, Sarah C., 29, 78
, Sophia J., 29, 78

McCall, Daniel A., 79
, Duncan, 46, 79
, Gilbert, 79, 97
, Hart, 53, 70, 82
, Joanna, 46, 47
, Paul, 8, 57
, Roderick, 79
, Roderick H. H. 79
McCormick, William, 26
McCracken, Allen M., 30
, Catherine, 79
, James (W.), 79
, John M., 79
, Mary, 79
, Spencer Y., 30
, Thomas C., 30
, Thomas E., 68
, William, 79
McCrary, Alexander, 30, 80
, Ann, 80
, Frances, 80
, James J., 30, 80
, Letha, 80
, Litha, 30
, Mary Ann, 30
, Rebecca, 30, 80
, Thomas, 30, 80
, Warren, 30, 80
McDonald, Angus R., 25
, Archibald, 56
, Celia Ann, 81
, Eufenia, 81
, John, 71, 81
, Mary, 81
, Neally, 81
, Sarah, 81
McGilvary, Anna, 32
, Duncan, 19, 82
, James 32
, John, 82
McGinty, Eliz. C., Mrs., 64
, George W., 17, 64
McInnis, Miles, 37
McIntosh, John D., 27
, Nancy A., 27
McKay, Winney, 81
McKee, Rachel M., 29
, William, 29
McKenzie, A., 82
, D. M., 62, 74
, Daniel, 4, 25, 37,
49, 74, 81
, John, 81

McKinney, A. F., 80
McKinny, Alexander, 30
   , Sarah, 30, 80
McLane, Hugh, 82
   , John, 82
   , Libby, 82
McLendon, John G., 27
McLeod, Daniel, 82
   , Frances L., 65
   , John, 56
   , Smitha, 82
   , William, 65
McLeroy, Emily, 91
   , John, 91
   , Martha G., 91
   , Mary, 91
   , Sarah, 91
   , W. H., 91
McMill(i)an, Charles, 31, 83
     , Edward, 31, 83
     , Fairly, 31, 83
     , Finlay, 31, 83
     , John, 31, 83
     , Mary, 31, 83
McNab, John, 68, 83
   , John C., 15, 19, 59, 79, 82
   , Lucy Ann, 85
McNair, John, 17
   , John P., 8, 21, 68, 77
   , Randall, 68
McNeil, Abigal, 32
McNeill, Anderson, 99
   , Angus, 32
   , Elizabeth, 99
   , John C., 101
   , Roderick, 32
McPhail, Edward C., 32, 50
McRae, Alexander, 81
   , Harvey A., 37, 90
   , John, 20
   , Lucy, 37, 90
McTyer, Robert A., 61
Meadley, Eldrige, 61
Mealing, John H., 88
Miles, Mary, 16
Miller, A. J. 14, 62
   , A. T., 44, 57
   , Asa T., 94
   , Elizabeth, 14, 62
   , John H., 33
Millsap, Emily E., 93

Millsap, T. C., 93
Minshew, Nathan, 16, 87, 100
Minter, Mariana S., 87
Mitchell, A. C., 12
   , Americus C., 71
   , Catherine, 71
   , Randolph, 83
   , Sarah G., 83
Moore, Americus, 32, 83
   , James P., 32, 83
   , Mary E., 32, 83, 84
   , William B., 32, 84
Morgan, Amanda, 20, 67
   , Charlotte, 24, 73
   , Littleton, 24, 73
   , Thomas, 20, 67
Morton, Lemuel B., 14
   , Sarah, 14
Mosely, F. M., 48
   , Mary Ann, 48
Moss, Malinda, 24
   , Temperance, 73
   , Uriah, 24, 73
Muncours, Sinthy, 66
Nance, Catherine, 87
   , Sylvester, 87
Nash, A. E., 84
   , Jacob B., 84
   , Margaretta, 84
   , Reubin A., 84
   , Thomas, 84
Neely, A. G., 20
   , Andrew G., 19, 44, 67, 77
   Louisa W., 19, 67
Nelson, Catherine (J.), 29, 78
   , Elizabeth, 33
   , Jacob, 29, 33, 78
   , James S., 33
   , John Gill, 33
Newton, Anderson, 85
   , Margaret, 85
   , Mary, 85
Nichols, Bass, 36
   , Emily, 2
Norris, Richard, 38
Norton, Amanda D., 33
   , Daniel A., 40, 47
   , Delila A., 33, 85
   , Erban W., 33
   , Franklin W., 33, 85
   , Isabella, 33
   , James R., 22, 33, 64, 69, 85

Norton, James W., 77
, John K., 82
, Lucinda K., 33
, Margaret, 22, 69
, Nancy A., 33, 85
, Thomas C., 33, 85
, Tolbot M., 85
, Tolbert W. M., 33
, Urban W., 85
Odom, Amelia, 85
, Catharine, 85
, Frances, 85
, Isabella, 85
, Peter, 85
, Robert, 85
, Thomas, 85
Oliver, A. Browder, 34
, Alexander B., 34
, A. R. 86
, Ann, 101
, Augustus L., 101
, E. E., 90
, Henry Y., 34, 86
, Jasper (N.), 34, 86
, M. D., 34
, McDonald, 34, 86
, Milbry, 34, 86
, William, 34, 86
Orr, James, 7, 28, 77
Osborn, Mills, 11
Owens, Fanny, 53
, Fanny Ann, 4
, John, 53
, T. C., 63
, Thadeus C., 16
Padget, Elijah, 37, 90
Paramore, John, 40
Parmer, Adeline, 2
, Jacob, 6, 50, 101
, Jacob, Jr., 52
Parrott, A. P., 79
Patterson, Barlett, 86
, Delany L. D., 86
, Julia A., 86
, Manerva C., 86
, Turner D., 86
, William C., 86
Paul, Hinson K., 48
, Rebecca (J.), 38, 99
Peacock, L. L., 24, 73
, Mary, 24, 73
Peake, John H., 34
, Virginia, 34, 86
Pearson, B. F., 4, 34

Perdue, Colly, 18
, Milly, 18
Perry, Mary C., 86
Persons, Clinton R., 34
Peterson, Batt, 19
Petty, B. F., 50
, Benj. F., 21, 34, 100
, Charles, 22, 27, 36, 47, 59
, N. A., 21, 85
Phillips, Caroline S., 35, 87
, Eaton, 58
, N. E. K., 35, 87
Pierce, L. L., 53
Pope, Cullen J., 38
Poston, Emanual, 85
Powell, Ann, 87
, Becky Ann, 87
, Caroline, 87
, Edy, 87
, Epsy, 87
, Joseph, 87
, Margaret, 87
, Matilda, 87
, Mary, 87
, Ransom, 87
, Sarah, 87
Pratt, Charles, 100
, Mary Jane, 100
Prescott, Mary, 2
Price, Celia, 22
, L. L., 53
, R. E., 22, 77
, Robert E., 28, 69
, Sealy, 69
, W. E., 102
, William E., 51
Pruett, James M., 10, 14, 31, 48
, John T., 88
, Josephine, 88
, Louisa, 14
Pugh, J. L., 82
, James L., 64
Pynes, Calista, 88
, Columbus, 88
, Daniel, 88
, Fair, 12, 60
, Francis M., 88
, John, 39
, Kitsy A., 39
, Lupyna, 88
, Lydia, 88
, Mary Ann, 88

Pynes, Melissa, 88
, Ruth, 88
, Thadeus, 88
Rachels, Hamlin, 32
, Sarah, 32
Rainey, H. W., 21
Rainy, Fedina, 84
, William, 84
Rawls, Kelly, 35, 35, 88
, Sally A., 35, 88
Ray, Polly, 100
Reaves, H. F., 6
, Harrell F., 28, 77
Reid, Caroline T., 89
, D. Turza, 35
, Dicy, 18
, James, 18
, James H., 35, 88
, Jane, 35, 89
, Josiah W., 35, 89
, Sophie T., 35, 88
, Terza C., 88
, Thomas D., 35, 88
, Wyatt, 89
Reynolds, George, 38, 92
, John A., 3, 67
, Letty Ann, 92
Rhea, Polly, 100
, Wilson, 100
Richards, Elizabeth C., 89
, James M., 89
, Martha A., 89
, Matilda, 89
, Robert J., 89
, Thomas J., 89
, Thomas W., 66
Richardson, James W., 35
, Walker, 23, 35
Ricks, John C., 58
, Polly, 58
Rist, Calvin, 47
Roberts, F. F., 36
, Francis P., 89
, John L., 34, 36, 86, 89
, Roberta, 36
, Sarah, 34, 86
, Thomas, 4, 36
Robertson, John W., 3
Robinson, Har(r)iet E., 4, 53
, John, 4, 53
, Thomas, 85
Rogers, William F., 93
Roquemore, Thomas J., 40, 94
Rouse, Ann (H.), 36, 89, 90

Rouse, Mary, 36, 89, 90
Rumley, Winney, 24, 71
Russell, Ellen S. A., 36
, Hartwell W., 36
, James H., 36
, Joseph C., 36, 98
, Joseph R., 36
, Lucius A., 36
, Ursuly, 36
, William R., 36
Ryan, Hampton, 52
Sapp, Margaret (A.), 35, 88
, William, 35, 88
Sasser, John, 65
Sauls, John, 37, 90
Saunders, Frances A., 39
, Joseph, 39
Sayres, Tobitha, 55
, William, 55
Scarborough, Francis, 90
, Hardy F., 90
Screws, Benjamin, 59
Scroggins, George R., 37, 71
Seals, D. M., 22, 54, 64, 94
, Daniel M., 27, 51, 59
60, 76, 86
, E. Jane, 14, 62
, John D., 14, 62
Shanks, George, 100
, James, 13
, James, Sr., 100
, Jeremiah, 13, 87
Sharp, James T., 90
, Judith H., 90
, Robert J., 90
, Sarah S., 90
Sheperd, John, 53
Molsey, 52, 53
Sheppard, Amy, 99, 100
, Annie, 100
, E., 48
, John, 99
Shipman, Alexander, 37, 90
, Benjamin F., 37, 91
, Eliza, 37, 90
, Elizabeth, 37
, George (L.), 37, 91
, James L., 37, 71, 76, 90
, Jesse, 37, 91
, Lewis, 37, 91
Shipp, Nancy, 15
, William, 15
Short, Richard V., 91
Shorter, Caroline, 91

Shorter, E. S., 13
, Eli S., 12, 33, 38
61, 84, 91
, Henry R., 38, 91
, James B., 91
, John Gill, 25, 31, 32,
38, 59, 80, 81,
83 91
, Laura M., 38
, Mary B., 38, 91
, Reubin C., 38, 91
, Reubin C., Jr., 91
, Sophia H., 38
Simpson, J. B., 71
, John D. T., 91
, Virginia, 91
Sinquefield, Moses, 38
Skains, Churren T., 49
Slack, Anna, 92
, David G., 92
, Frances, 92
, Francis, 38
, J. B., 92
, Jacob, 92
, James, 38, 92
, Jesse, 12, 38, 92
, John, 38, 92
, Mary, 38
, Mary Ann, 92
, Thomas, 92
Sloan, David, 44, 95
, John, 26
Smart, Cleopatra, 46, 47
, Thomas S., 9, 34, 40,
46,47, 57, 97
Smith, Barbara, 84
, Benjamin F., 9
, Elizabeth, 29, 78
, Isaiah, 66
, James B. R., 84
, Jane, 2
, John W., 90
, N. N. Dr., 78
, Sarah A., 38
, Sidney A., 9, 58
, William S., 49
, Young, 40
Smitha, William, 48
Snead, Daniel B., 33
, Elizabeth C., 33
Sneed, M. J., Mrs., 3
Spear, David, 39
, Harriet, 30
, Henry G., 39, 92

Spear, William, 39, 92
, Willis M., 39
Spence, A. T., 36
Stanford, Elenor, 89
, Monroe, 89
Stanley, Elizabeth J., 93
, James G., 93
, John W., 93
, Parmenas B., 93
, Sarah W., 93
, Sherwood L., 93
, William L., 93
, William M., 93
Starke, A. B., 63
, E. W., 63
, Eli W., 16, 63
, Frances C., 63
, J. M., 16
Stembridge, John A., 39, 93
, Sarah E., 39, 93
Stephens, Calvin, 55
, Eliza, 55
, Epsey D., 39
, Green, 39, 79
, Isabel C., 39
, Nancy A., 39
, Peletia G., 38
, Sarah E., 39
, William W., 90
Sterns, Jane, 99
, W. H., 99
Stewart, Alexander, 94
, Daniel L., 94
, Jane, 94
, John L., 88, 94
, Norman, 37
, Peter, 81
Stinson, George, 25
Stokes, James W., 75
, Martha A., 75
Stovall, Cicero, 40, 94
, George (W.), 40, 94
, Mary, 40, 94
Streeter, B. F. 67
, M. H., 92
, S. M., 67
, Sheppard M., 5
Stringer, Emma L., 94
, James A., Jr., 94
, Lilly, 94
, Sarah (A.), 40, 94
Sylvester, Mary, 34
, Thomas R., 3, 11
Tarver, Benjamin H., 95

Tate, Cynthia, 40
Taylor, Jesse, 65
    , M. S., 63
    , Samual J., 74
Tew, Peter, 53
Thally, Susannah, 13
Tharp, Elizabeth, 2
Thomas, Aaron, 41, 42
    , Charity, 41
    , David, 55
    , Eli, 41
    , Elizabeth, 1, 55
    , Elliott, 8, 41, 42, 56
    , Federick P., 11
    , George H., 8, 41, 95
    , James E., 41
    , Jane, 41
    , Jonathan, 7, 8, 41, 42
            43, 56, 95
    , Joseph, 41
    , Maria J., 7
    , Mariah J., 8
    , Martha S., 98
    , Mary A., 11
    , Mary F., 8, 41
    , Mary P., 95
    , Morgan, 67
    , Retensey, 8
    , Ruth C., 8, 56
    , Sally, 99
    , Sarah Jane, 41
    , William, 1, 99
    , William B., 41
    , Z. Taylor, 42
    , Zachariah T., 8, 41, 95
Thomason, Gideon Y., 93
Thompson, Adam C., 42, 95
    , Aladen, 42
    , David A., 25, 74
    , Enoch, 42
    , Frances, 25, 74
    , George H., 35
    , James M., 49
    , John, 42
    , Louisa H., 35
    , Lucinda, 16
    , Rhoda, 42
    , Robert, 42
    , Sarah, 42
    , Thomas, 42
    , William, 16, 42
Thornton, Edward Q., 42, 95
    , Green H., 9
    , J. M., 4

Thornton, Joseph B., 42, 95
    , Mary B., 38, 61
    , Rosolva D., 9
    , W. H., 42, 91, 95
    , William H., 11
Tinsley, A. A., 43, 93
    , Albert, 43
    , Albina, 43
    , Charles, 43, 93
    , Fanny, 43
    , James, 43
    , Julia, 43
    , Leven A. A., 93
    , Lucy, 43
    , Sarah, 43
Tison, James G., 35, 88
Todd, Jahazo, 10
    , William, 10
Tompkins, H. M., 33, 34, 42
Toombs, G., 23, 35
Townsend, S. J., 85
Trammell, Ann P., 43
    , Ann P. J., 95
    , Daniel M., 9, 43, 95
    , Eliza J., 43, 95
    , James, 43
    , John H., 43, 95
    , Mary Jane, 9
Truetlin, Caroline, 44
    , Cornelia, 44, 95, 96
    , John (F.), 44, 96
    , Julia, 44, 95, 96
    , Mary A., 44, 95, 96
    , Sarah, 44, 95, 96
    , Sarah, 44, 95, 96
Turk, George W., 44, 96
    , Lillis A., 44
Turman, George J., 72
    , James M., 44
Turnage, Carney, 44
    , Eliza, 58
Turner, Caroline E., 45, 96
    , James K., 62
    , John R., 96
    , John W., 45
    , Noel W., 45, 96
Upshaw, Eugenia, 45
    , Leroy, 45, 96
    , Maria G., 45, 96
    , William T., 45, 96
Urquhart, Henry N., 66
Utsey, A. F., 98
    , Absolem F., 47
    , Jacob, 82

117

Utsey, Mary, 98
　　, Mary E., 47
Vann, Edward W., 45
　　, Henry M., 46
　　, Joseph L., 45, 96
　　, Joseph M., 46
　　, Sarah, 45, 96
Varnadore, Isham, 55
　　　, Nancy, 55
　　　, Susan, 55
　　　, Thomas, 55
Ventress, James, 101
　　　Thomas, 101
Vickers, Thomas T. B., 50
Vinning, Ann, 78
　　, Anna, 30
　　, David (J.), 30, 78
　　, Eliza (J.), 30, 78
　　, George (B.), 30, 78
　　, Jackson (L.), 30, 78
　　, Jane, 29, 78
　　, Mary (A.), 29, 78
　　, Samuel, 29, 78
　　, Sarah (A.), 30, 78
　　, Washington, 30, 78
　　, William, 30
　　, William M., 78
Vorhees, Cornelius, 2
Waddy, James E., 23
Walkley, James C., 11
Walkly, Selden S., 38
Wall, Josiah, 16
Wallace, W. D., 85
Walton, Jeremiah, 29, 78
　　, Sarah, 29, 78
Ward, Henry C., 97
　　, Julia Ann, 46
　　, L. D., 46, 47
　　, Lewis D., 46
Warren, A. J., 46
　　, Adeline, 46, 47, 97
　　, America, 46, 97
　　, Bates, 46, 47, 97
　　, Burris, 46, 47, 97
　　, Cenia, 46
　　, E. K. P., 46, 47, 97
　　, Georgeanna, 46, 47, 97
　　, H. M., 51
　　, J. D., 51, 97
　　, Jackson L., 47, 97
　　, James, 99
　　, James E., 47, 48, 98, 99
　　, Joel, 99

Warren, Joel D., 47, 48, 97, 98
　　, Joseph M., 47, 98
　　, Julia, 47
　　, Lucinda, 46, 47, 96, 97
　　, Martha, 98
　　, Milly L., 47
　　, Monroe, 46, 47, 97
　　, Rebecca, 47, 98
　　, Sarah, 46, 97, 99
　　, Sarah A., 97
　　, Susan, 47, 98, 99
　　, Thomas E., 46, 47, 97
　　, Thomas J., 98
　　, Thomas M., 47, 98, 99
Watkins, James W., 84
Watson, Daniel G., 48, 99
　　, Elizabeth, 28, 48, 99
　　, George L., 28
　　, James, 74
　　, James F. M., 48, 99
　　, James Francis, 48
　　, Jesse Z., 48, 99
　　, John, 7
　　, John J., 48, 99
　　, M. M., 7, 22, 69
　　, Mary, 7
　　, Nathan C., 48, 99
　　, Patience, 22, 69
　　, Peter W., 48, 99
　　, Thomas J., 48
Weathers, Jane, 99
　　　, Patsey, 99, 100
　　　, Samuel, 99, 100
　　　, Solomon, 99
　　　, William, 99
Webb, Rachel J., 4, 53
　　, W. S., 4, 53
　　, William S., 4
Weldon, W. A., 63
Wellborn, Carlton, 48
　　　, Johnson, 45
　　　, Lucy F., 48
　　　, M. B., 48
　　　, Mary A., 48
West, Joseph, 59
Westbrook, John M., 70
　　　, Sarah Ann, 70
Wheatly, Rhoda, 92
　　　, Samuel G., 92
White, Gamville, 48
　　, John M., 65

White, R. T., 66, 88
    , Robert T., 85
    , Willis, 38
Whitehurst, Asa, 49, 100
      , George Ann, 100
      , Levi, 100
      , Mary Ann, 49, 100
      , Mary B., 49, 100
Whitsett, Catherine, 32
    , Samuel, 32
Wiley, D. J. B., 49
    , James McCaleb, 49
    , Leroy, 49
    , Thomas H., 49
Wilkinson, Henry T., 75
      , John O. C., 53
      , W. W., 75
Wilks, Jesse, 26
Williams, Arincey, 8
    , B., 9, 18, 57
    , B. F., 101
    , Betsy Ann, 50
    , Braddock, 50
    , Buckner, 38, 66, 101
    , Columbianna, 8, 49
    , E. C., 50, 101
    , Effy, 32, 50, 83
    , Elender, 50
    , Elizabeth, 22, 69
    , G. W., 49
    , Isabella, 50
    , J. S., 70, 101
    , James, 101
    , Jane A., 8, 49
    , Jere N. 101, 102
    , John D., 27
    , John L., 100
    , Louisianna, 8, 49
    , M. A., Mrs., 101
    , Mary A., 8, 49
    , Mary C., 50
    , Mary O., 100
    , Samuel L., 101
    , Sarah, 50
    , Sarah E., 8, 49
    , Sophia, 101
    , Wiley, 50
    , William, 7, 22, 49
        50, 69
    , Z. C., 10
Williamson, Faithy Ann, 55
    , William, 55

Willis, Sarah A. S., 40
Wilson, Nancy, 2
Windham, Anthony, 7, 15
    , Epsey, 15
Witherington, Robert, 57
Wood, Cynth(i)a, 49, 100
    , James, 49, 100
    , William, 58
Woodall, Jonathan, 100
      , Margaret, 100
      , Peggy, 100
Woods, E. P., 78
Worthington, Robert, 9
Wray, Margaret, 16
    , Raiford, 16
Wright, R. S., 92
    , Richard S., 5
Yarrington, R. J., 97
Young, Edward B., 52